D0800534

SMS Uprising

Mobile Phone Activism in Africa

Edited by Sokari Ekine

Pambazuka Press
An imprint of Fahamu Books

Published 2010 by Pambazuka Press, an imprint of Fahamu Books
Cape Town, Dakar, Nairobi and Oxford
www.pambazukapress.org   www.fahamubooks.org   www.pambazuka.org

Fahamu, 2nd floor, 51 Cornmarket Street, Oxford OX1 3HA, UK
Fahamu Kenya, PO Box 47158, 00100 GPO, Nairobi, Kenya
Fahamu Senegal, 9 Cité Sonatel 2, POB 25021, Dakar-Fann, Dakar, Senegal
Fahamu South Africa, c/o 27A Esher St, Claremont, 7708,
Cape Town, South Africa

First published 2010

British Library Cataloguing in Publication Data
A catalogue record for this book is available from the British Library

ISBN: 978-1-906387-35-8 paperback

ISBN: 978-1-906387-36-5 ebook

Publication of this book was made possible with the support
of a grant from HIVOS.

Manufactured on demand by Lightning Source

Contents

About the contributors

Redante Asuncion-Reed is a blogger and writer who lives in Washington DC, in the United States. He wrote the original version of Chapter 5 as his master's thesis for the graduate programme in public communication at American University in 2007.

Amanda Atwood is information and content manager at Kubatana.net in Zimbabwe.

Ken Banks is the founder of kiwanja.net and the developer of FrontlineSMS. He specialises in the application of mobile technology for positive social and environmental change in the developing world. He combines over 25 years in IT with over 16 years experience living and working throughout Africa.

Christiana Charles-Iyoha is a development policy analyst with a particular interest in gender influence, coherence and integration in development. She is the executive director of PolDeC, an NGO based in Lagos, and is an active participant in the Nigerian and global social development discourse. She contributed a chapter to Tactical Technology Collective's Mobiles in-a-box.

Nathan Eagle is an Omidyar fellow at the Santa Fe Institute. His research involves engineering computational tools, designed to explore how large-scale human behavioural data can be used for social good. He is the founder of txteagle.

Sokari Ekine is an activist with a multidisciplinary background in technology, education and human rights. She has a postgraduate degree in human rights and education and has worked in education and several online publications including Pambazuka News. She is author of the blog Black Looks.

Becky Faith works with Tactical Tech and led the development of the Mobiles in-a-box project. She is an experienced producer and technologist who has worked in new media production since 1995. She is passionate about the potential of mobile phones in advocacy and campaigning and has implemented a number of projects using mobile technology for campaigning in Africa, including the Global Call to Action against Poverty.

Joshua Goldstein is a technology consultant and writer living in New York City. He primarily helps international organisations and companies find opportunities in Africa's emerging mobile and web business and policy landscape. He currently works with UNICEF Innovations and Appfrica Labs while blogging here and tweeting @african_minute. While completing his masters degree at the Fletcher School, Tufts University, he worked with Google Inc. on technology policy in Africa and with Harvard's Berkman Center for Internet & Society, exploring the effect of internet on democracy.

Christian Kreutz is a political scientist and knowledge activist. He currently works as a consultant for information and communication technologies for development (ICT4D). He worked for five years as a project manager with the GTZ – German Technical Cooperation, and as a communication and learning specialist in Egypt and Germany. He blogs at www.crisscrossed.net.

Anil Naidoo is an advocate of the High Court of South Africa. He was the UmNyango project manager. He heads the Indiba-Africa Group of which Indiba-Africa Consulting and Indiba-Africa Media are subsidiaries. The Group supports social justice through the work of the Indiba-Africa Development Alliance (www.indiba-africa.org.za; www.indiba-africa.mobi) and the South Africa Coalition for the International Criminal Court.

Berna Ngolobe is advocacy officer in the Gender and ICT Policy Advocacy Programme with the Women of Uganda Network (WOUGNET). WOUGNET was established by several women's organisations in Uganda to develop the use of ICTs among women for sustainable national development.

Tanya Notley is a social researcher who currently provides skills-building support to a number of Tactical Technology's mobile and advocacy projects. She has more than ten years experience working with research institutes, international development agencies and community-based organisations in Australia, the UK, Nepal, India and Sri Lanka. Tanya has a PhD in Media and Communications from Queensland University of Technology.

Juliana Rotich is the programme director of Ushahidi.com, an innovative non-profit web start-up that creates software for mapping crises. In addition to her role at Ushahidi, she is a blogger,

Introduction

Sokari Ekine

As a blogger using the web as an agent of social change, I find the growth of mobile phone use in Africa offers an opportunity to look at the innovative ways this emerging technology is being used by grassroots groups and small and micro NGOs across the continent. I was very pleased to be invited to edit this book by Fahamu as it provided a chance to explore this potential, looking at not only the positives but also the negatives in order to expose the underlying reality. *SMS Uprising* is significant for many reasons not least because it has been edited by an African woman activist. Often initiatives in Africa are studied by people who are quite distant from the continent or are academics who are remote from the grassroots of the subject under discussion. The book is also unique in giving an insight into how activists and social change advocates are addressing Africa's many challenges from within, and how they are using mobile telephone technology to facilitate these changes. The examples are shared in such a way that they can be easily replicated – 'pick this idea up and use it in your campaign!' The intention is that the information contained within the book will lead to greater reflection about the real potential and limitations of mobile technology. The protests following the Iranian elections, the Mumbai bombings and the G20 summit in London, in which mobile phones played a central role in organising, mobilising, communicating and disseminating information across the world in real time, show the actual and potential power of citizens' journalism in times of crisis. One single message sent by SMS to Twitter can spread throughout the world in minutes.

For a social justice activist, such research is important not only to understanding the overall technology landscape but also in providing a chance to contribute to a movement that acknowledges and tackles potential problems while interrogating its strengths. There is no doubt that mobile and internet technology is democratising social change in communities across Africa. We must, however, also recognise that technology has the capacity to concentrate power and therefore could be used to reinforce existing power relations.

The introduction of mobile phones in Africa transforms people's ability to communicate. Unlike in the West, where there was already an existing network of communication through landlines, mobile phones in Africa provide communication where previously there was none. In 2007, it was estimated that there were 300 million mobile phone users – about 30 per cent[1] of the continent's population.[2] Whilst mobile phone usage continues to grow exponentially[3] and in some countries has reached critical mass, a more discerning reading of the figures is necessary to obtain a picture of the reality. This kind of examination helps to explain why and how mobile phones have been used for social change in some instances and countries, and not in others. For example, the figures do not reveal the number of handsets per person nor, conversely, how many people are sharing one handset. People at upper-income levels particularly, tend to have two phones on different networks and, in some cases, even three or four.

There are also some huge discrepancies between regions and countries as well as within countries – such as between rural and urban populations. The report titled 'Mobile telephony access and usage in Africa' shows this clearly. For example, the 2008 subscriber rates for South Africa (87.08 per cent) are around three times that of Nigeria (27.28 per cent) and Kenya (30.48 per cent). Ethiopia is only 1.45 per cent and Rwanda 6.53 per cent.[4] What does seem to affect the diffusion of mobile phone use, as Nathan Eagle points out in Chapter 1, 'Economics and power within the African telecommunication industry', is whether or not the telecommunications industry is deregulated. So, for instance, in Uganda where there is much competition, prices are low, while Ethiopia, which remains highly regulated with no competition, has high calling costs.

Technology in itself does not lead to social change. For change to take place technology needs to be appropriate and rooted in local knowledge. People decide why and how a particular technology will be used and, depending on the political and socio-economic environment in which they live, adapt it accordingly. As we shall see from the case studies in this book, there are considerable local innovations and non-instrumental uses of the phone – using phones in ways not intended, that step outside their technological aspects and which attempt to bypass traditional power structures. Firoze Manji describes this process as ordinary people taking control of their destiny rather than technology driving the change:

> Social change is actually driven not by technologies but by ordinary people being able to exert an authority over their own experience and, through common actions, developing the courage to determine their own destiny.[5]

It is important in the context of this book to point out that the projects and innovations discussed within it do not follow a traditional development model, where technology tends to be shaped by the economic forces that created it. Instead, the social change model is driven by the forces of people's local needs and is therefore more able to respond quickly and appropriately to specific events and political changes. This means that people at a grass-roots level can think about what works for them and how can they use technology to foster social change and collective action.

What makes the mobile phone such a dynamic tool for supporting social change is its sheer range of actual and potential functionality, making it an extremely versatile technology. Erik Hersman, who authors the leading blog on high-tech mobile and web technology change in Africa (White African and the Africa Network: An Idea by Erik Hersman), coined the phrase, 'If it works in Africa it will work anywhere', referring to Africa's many innovative ideas, projects and people.[6] Activists and campaign groups have also chosen to use mobile phones – SMS and video – for mobilising, advocacy, campaigning, social networking, citizens' journalism and crowdsourcing.[7] Campaigns can be short or long term and planned in advance, but quite often they are spontaneously reacting to an event. For example:

- The International Center for Accelerated Development (ICAD) in Nigeria used mobile phones to bring people together for a rally during the Global AIDS Week of Action campaign, which began in April 2008. ICAD Nigeria also used SMS to mobilise supporters in the Plateau State elections in 2008[8] (see Chapter 4 of this book).
- In 2007 WOUGNET in Uganda used SMS as part of the 16 Days of Activism to End Violence Against Women campaign. 170 messages were sent out in 13 countries across four continents[9] (see Chapter 8).
- In Egypt, activists have used both SMS and the video cameras on their mobile phones to mobilise and expose police torture. One particularly harrowing video showed a 13-year-old boy, Mohammed Mamdouh Abdel Aziz, being tortured by the police. Using video and testimonies, activists have been able to document torture in Egypt thereby giving their claims real credibility.[10]

However SMS or the phone in general is not always the most effective or appropriate technology as Bukeni Waruzi's paper (see Chapter 11) on using mobiles in the DRC shows – in a crisis writing an SMS takes time. It is far quicker to make a voice call. In another example, the UmNyango project (see Chapter 6) found that women preferred to report domestic violence face to face rather using a phone.

Varying examples must be seen in the context of local infrastructures which impact on usage but at the same time lead to technological and non-technological innovations to overcome constraints. In fact, mobile phones have led to a huge growth in the informal sector with entrepreneurs who support usage such as selling airtime, selling chargers, charging, recycling and repairing phones – nothing is left to waste.[11]

This book aims to provide an examination of the many inventive ways that activism and social change are taking place across Africa and how mobile phones have been co-opted as the primary tool to aid this process. My own research in compiling this book's chapters leads me to consider a number of questions regarding the context of technology in Africa. For example, who is a user and who is an owner? To what extent are these projects and innovations breaking down traditional and capitalistic hierarchies? How have activists been able to use the technology to really affect change? Is access to a mobile phone and using it for social change more than just a drop in the ocean? Where people use technology to advance movement for change and to empower communities in putting forward information about human rights abuses, electoral abuses, empowering women, etc, are these changes actually sustainable? Given that women are largely responsible for development, particularly in rural areas, and how under-resourced women are, what kind of a resource does a mobile phone give them? From observing and talking to women in Nigeria, it is clear that the purchase of airtime was given a high priority but was also used with much caution. The main complaints were always the cost of airtime and poor reception. This led to people wanting to own more than one handset from different networks – another additional cost. On the other hand, as Christiana Charles-Iyoha points out in Chapter 9, the high level of poverty amongst women undermines women's role in development and socio-economic transformation as they are excluded from owning a phone and their status often limits even the sharing of a phone within the family.

Another constraint that particularly impacts on women, due to their overwhelming poverty, is the poor electricity supply, which means that to be effective there is a need for two phones. Nonetheless, at least one report found that there was no difference in how men and women used mobile phones and in fact in some situations phones decreased the isolation of women and increased job creation for those selling airtime and other related products.[12]

It would be unethical to write about mobile phones in general, and particularly in an African context, without mentioning the mining of coltan, which is an essential element in the production of the phones. In a report in the UK daily newspaper the *Independent*, Johann Hari makes a direct link between the increase in deaths and the mining of coltan in the Kivu province of the Democratic Republic of Congo (DRC), naming Anglo-America, Standard Chartered Bank, De Beers and more than 100 others involved.[13] We should therefore be mindful when we read of the huge growth in mobile phone usage on the continent of the major cost in lives and human rights abuses associated with the mining of coltan.

The projects in this book are reliant on external funding and, in many cases, support from multinational service providers seeking profit. By funding mobile phone-based projects, these companies believe that users will want to add value for themselves by using the phone as a general means of communicating, thereby offsetting costs of the funding. But if pricing of airtime and handsets is too high, this may not happen or only in a limited way. Finally, we should approach the technology carefully, as there are pitfalls. For example, by ignoring traditional forms of communication and indigenous forms of organising, people, especially women, can end up being disempowered.

The contributors to this book have been chosen because they offer a comprehensive range of experiences drawn from across the continent. Every attempt has been made to include a variety of voices – activists, organisations, academics and technologists – which provides a range of perspectives in addressing the issues raised above.

Part I provides the political, economic and technological context. Contributors examine the political economy of the telecommunications industry and discuss the possibilities and constraints on future developments and how mobile phones are used. Nathan Eagle (see Chapter 1) offers an overview of the economics and politics of the African telecommunications industry. Not surprisingly, and despite the rapid decline in airtime costs, the mobile phone market in Africa reaps huge profits. China's position in the market is considerable and in the case of Ethiopia they have taken over the whole telecoms equipment industry. One result has been high airtime costs as well as attacks on personal freedoms in the country. Eagle also discusses the privacy implications of monitoring the data produced by millions of mobile phones:

> Beyond documentation of voice and text-message communication and location estimates based on cellular towers, occasionally mobile operators have additional data about their subscribers, including demographic information, socio-economic status…

With mobile phones being used to transfer medical data including HIV/AIDS statistics and personal drug regimes, as well as human rights activists using phones for mobilisation and communication, the implications for data privacy, especially in repressive regimes, is worrying.

Christian Kreutz in Chapter 2 analyses future trends for mobile activism and social change in Africa and identifies four potential growth areas. However, he notes that there remain many technological and infrastructural challenges. These include the plethora of low cost phones with few features, which makes internet integration very much a thing of the future. Although airtime and hardware costs have reduced over the past five years, they still remain high enough to present obstacles to the majority of Africans. Kreutz introduces a range of mobile applications and discusses the realities of implementation given the many obstacles. He concludes that technology should only be used if it is appropriate and is the best option, rather than for its own sake.

Ken Banks is the founder of FrontlineSMS, which he describes as 'a piece of free software which turns a laptop (or desktop) computer, a mobile phone and a cable into a two-way group messaging centre'.

The focus of Banks's Chapter 3 'Social mobile: empowering the many or the few?' is the need to develop mobile applications for grassroots NGOs and thereby avoid creating yet another North/South divide. This means using a development model focused on creating tools that are available to everyone. Mobile technology solutions should be simple, appropriate and affordable, rather than top–down and capital intensive. This approach creates huge technical, economic and cultural challenges to developers, but is not impossible if one chooses to work with local communities and focus on empowering them.

A book on mobile phones and activism would not be complete without a detailed example of at least one technology tool and a description of the processes behind its ideas and development. Part I concludes with Chapter 4 by Tanya Notley and Becky Faith from the Tactical Technology Collective. Tactical Tech was formed in 2003 with the aim of bringing together the 'innovative activities' of human rights advocates in marginalised communities and the open source software movement. Despite being 'philosophically aligned' there was little interaction between the two, and the challenge for Tactical Tech was to develop appropriate, open source technology through collaboration with frontline human rights advocates. The chapter discusses the development of one particular toolkit, the Mobiles in-a-box, which is a collection of tools, tactics and guides on how mobile phone technology can be used for campaigns and advocacy. The processes described are a useful model for organisations wishing to embark on a participatory development approach towards social change and activism, with or without the application of technology.

Part II, 'Mobile democracy: SMS case studies', consists of practical examples of social change and mobile activism across the continent. The examples vary considerably, from SMS campaigns for a specific purpose to a more generalised use of SMS for advocacy or election monitoring, as an information tool to empower civil society, as a means of social intervention or to monitor and document crises.

In 2004 Fahamu ('an African activist organisation working for human rights and social justice') launched a campaign to promote the ratification of the Protocol of the Rights of Women in Africa. In 2005, they then launched another campaign in support of the Global Call to Action against Poverty. The use of SMS in both these campaigns was a strategic choice for Fahamu, who recognised the huge growth in mobile phones (52–67 million at the time of both campaigns) and the potential SMS had for mobilising social justice campaigns.

Redante Asuncion-Reed (Chapter 5) looks at, analyses and assesses both Fahamu campaigns. How we measure and define success is an important issue in any campaign and there is a tendency to focus too strictly on numerical data. Asuncion-Reed makes the point that both campaigns were measured by their consequences and were driven by achieving goals rather than by the number of people who responded through the technology. He then attempts to answer the question as to whether the campaigns achieved their stated goals of mobilising 'public pressure' for the ratification of the Protocol on African Women's Rights and to bring attention to the issue of global poverty.

Violence against women takes place across the world. However, in South Africa it has been aggravated by apartheid, which created a culture of aggression and brutality. The situation is further exacerbated by local patriarchies which discriminate against women in the areas of widowhood, land rights and inheritance laws. Despite constitutional protections in the post-apartheid South Africa, violence against women continues.

> As most studies show, violence against women is a multi-linked variable connecting to, inter alia, patriarchal 'configuration' of our society, poverty, illiteracy and general economic exclusion of women, especially African women. Poverty and economic exclusion results in unequal gender relations between men and women which in most cases translate into vulnerability in various ways.[14]

The UmNyango project (see Chapter 6) sought to address the twin issues of domestic violence and land exclusions. This was done by taking an integrated approach towards providing rural women in KwaZulu Natal (KZN) with timely and relevant information on human rights as well as access to a simple but effective reporting mechanism. UmNyango project manager, Anil Naidoo, examines the potential and limitations of SMS as a tool to empower rural women in KZN. Naidoo's contribution highlights the point that although technology might be more efficient and present more timely information, it is not necessarily the most appropriate in all situations. This is particularly pertinent to women living under patriarchal systems where they are treated as 'perpetual minors'. In the case of the women in the UmNyango project, they preferred face-to-face communication when discussing or reporting domestic violence. Other points raised in this chapter are the prohibitive costs attached to mobile phone use and the associated sustainability of funded projects.

The continued political and economic crisis in Zimbabwe has meant that the average Zimbabwean has very limited access to information – especially independent news media. Amanda Atwood explores the ways Kubatana has used mobile activism in a variety of campaigns, including during the 2008 Zimbabwean elections (Chapter 7). Kubatana has been at the forefront of developing innovative social and technological solutions to information scarcity and advocacy in repressive political environments. For example, Kubatana's mobile activism is informed by the exchange of ideas and by fostering two-way communication with Zimbabweans from all walks of life. Another exciting innovation she mentions is the development of the Freedom Fone. One of its features is the capability to go beyond the 160 character limit of SMS. The phone also enables communities to create their own content based on demand as it marries radio-style programming with both mobiles and landline phones. The Freedom Fone is significant not only because of this feature, but also as it is a technology developed in Africa in a country that has been in crisis for the past nine years and where most resources are extremely limited. Another important element of the Freedom Fone is that the idea and development have been led by Kubatana's technical director, Brenda Burrell.

WOUGNET (Women of Uganda Network) was started in 2000 and is one of the oldest NGOs working with women and ICT in Africa. WOUGNET's approach to gender and technology is driven by gender inequalities in both urban and rural women's status as well as in access to ICT, including mobile phones. The network participated in global and African SMS campaigns to raise awareness of violence against women in 2007 and 2008 (http://tinyurl.com/8kaubh), to provide timely agricultural information and to support online discussions on women's rights and development. Berna Ngolobe, in Chapter 8, offers a gender dimension to the use of ICT including SMS as a way of improving capacity and generally empowering women. She raises issues of patriarchy which lead to women experiencing real disadvantage in education and economic security. Both of these factors impact on women's access to mobile phones and therefore to participating in SMS-supported advocacy and campaign projects. Nonetheless, Uganda, which is also one of the countries involved in the Village Phone Initiative (http://tinyurl.com/qqd7ks), has taken a liberalised approach to telecommunications which has also led to increased access for women. This has resulted in a plethora of mobile service providers and one of the lowest call prices on the continent, thereby reducing some of the gender barriers that exist elsewhere in Africa.

In 'Mobile telephony: closing the gap' (Chapter 9), Christiana Charles-Iyoha, whilst recognising the pervasiveness of mobile phones and the innovative opportunities they have created, avoids the temptation to assert that we are moving towards a 'digitopia' particularly where women are concerned. Her chapter addresses gender imbalances, noting that women are largely excluded from accessing mobile phone technology and therefore from engaging actively in the development and social change process. She suggests a number of ways in which these inequalities can be addressed. By examining the factors that create obstacles she presents a number of practical ways of addressing imbalances.

Within 24 hours of the outbreak of the 2008/2009 post election violence in Kenya, Kenyan blogs were posting hour-by-hour reports. On 31 December, there was a complete shutdown of the mainstream media. Erik Hersman of 'White African' said:

> The only way to get any up-to-date news for the past 24–48 hours has been through the blogosphere (like Kenyan Pundit, Thinkers Room, Mentalacrobatics), Skype and Kenyan-populated forums (like Mashada). The traditional media has been shut out and shut down for all intents and purposes.[15]

Within days, the online community and blog aggregator, Mashada, had set up an SMS and voice hotline calling for people to send in local news and opinions on what was happening. This was followed by Ory Okolloh (Kenyan Pundit) who suggested using Google Earth to create a mashup[16] of where the violence was taking place and called upon 'any techies' out there willing to help create a map of it. This was 3 January and by 9 January a group of Kenyan bloggers had put together a mashup and created Ushahidi, a site for people to send SMS or email reports of acts of violence directly. What the Ushahidi project shows is that if you build a strong community then it is easier to come together in a time of crisis and take action.

Why was the Kenyan blogosphere able to rally in such a positive and productive way in such a short time? What can we learn from their actions that will help others deal with local crisis? These are some of the questions, Juliana Rotich and Joshua Goldstein address in 'Digitally networked technology' (Chapter 10).

Bukeni Waruzi's chapter provides an overview of the use of mobile phones for monitoring and reporting abuses of children's rights. The Kalundu Child Soldier project used members of local communities including some former child soldiers to monitor and report acts of violence such as from rape, torture and forced marriage. The project is based in the Kivu region of eastern Congo, which is the centre of the violence in the country as militias, multinationals and governments all vie for control of the rich mineral resources such as coltan. It is ironic that the main mineral required to manufacture the mobile phones being used to report human rights abuses is the very mineral which is causing the conflict in the first place.

The contributors in this book come from a variety of occupational backgrounds, a fact that is reflected in the different writing styles and approaches to the usefulness of mobile technology as a tool for social change and advocacy in Africa. While they are all aware of the need to overcome infrastructural, economic and cultural obstacles, they also have a strong desire for social change and have the vision to see what could be possible and how best to achieve this. We are facing increasing amplification of social differentiation – the rich continue to get richer and the poor, poorer. In the face of this inequality mobile phone activism in Africa, as examined in this book, emerges as a powerful force for achieving social justice.

Mobile phones as tools for social change and advocacy are at a relatively early stage of development, but that are growing at an exponential rate, and it is quite possible that within two years the whole landscape will have changed. There are, of course, many other innovative projects and ideas which could have been included if space permitted. There is also the need for more research to fill the vacuum of information that exists such as from North Africa, Egypt and other non-English speaking countries. I am quite confident that there will be an academic exploration of some of the experiences discussed in the book. *SMS Uprising* is offered as the beginning, and showcases positive examples of what is possible and what can inspire people to use technology to support their actions.

Compiling this book has been a learning experience for me both as an editor and in terms of understanding how mobile telephony is being used in Africa. It has also been a privilege to work with Fahamu, who have been supportive and patient throughout.

Notes

1. Obtaining accurate and timely figures for Africa's mobile telephones is not a precise task as numbers and percentage figures differ, though only marginally. At the end of 2007 there were 280.7 million mobile phone

subscribers in Africa, representing a penetration rate of 30.4 per cent (from approximately 50 million, or 10 per cent penetration, in 2002). This is set to reach 580 million and a penetration rate of 95 per cent by 2012. http://whiteafrican.com/2008/08/01/2007-african-mobile-phone-statistics/, accessed 15 May 2009.

2. (2008) 'African mobile subscribers surpass North America', Textually.org, http://www.textually.org/textually/archives/2008/05/019983.htm, accessed 15 May 2009.
3. Hash (2008) '2007 mobile phone statistics', White African http://whiteafrican.com/2008/08/01/2007-african-mobile-phone-statistics/, accessed 15 May 2009.
4. Hash (2009) 'Mobile telephony access and usage in Africa', White African, http://whiteafrican.com/wp-content/uploads/2009/04/researchictafrica-ictd2009.pdf, accessed 27 May 2009.
5. Manji, F. (2008) 'Mobile activism, mobile hype', *Gender and Media Diversity Journal*, no. 4, January, pp. 125–32, http://www.genderlinks.org.za/page.php?p_id=398, accessed 14 September 2009.
6. Hash (2008) 'If it works in Africa, it will work anywhere', White African, http://whiteafrican.com/2008/09/26/if-it-works-in-africa-it-will-work-anywhere/, accessed 15 May 2009.
7. Crowdsourcing – When citizens working as a collective report on a crisis with real-time news from a particular region or on a particular situation we can call it 'crowdsourcing in citizen journalism'.
8. Tactical Tech 'Using mobile phones to monitor local elections', Tactical Technology Collective, http://wiki.mobiles.tacticaltech.org/index.php/Using_mobile_phones_to_monitor_local_elections, accessed 27 May 2009.
9. WOUGNET (2008) '16 Days Of Activism: SMS campaign 2008', http://www.wougnet.org/cms/index.php?option=com_content&task=view&id=315&Itemid=29, accessed 15 May 2009.
10. Tactical Tech 'Exposing police torture with mobile phone video', Tactical Technology Collective, http://www.mobiles.tacticaltech.org/Exposingpolicetorturewithmobilephonevideo, accessed 15 May 2009.
11. Banks, K. (2008) 'Build it Kenny, and they will come... Mobile telephony and the entrepreneur', http://www.kiwanja.net/blog/2008/10/mobile-telephony-and-the-entrepreneur/, accessed 27 May 2009.
12. Nthateng, M. (2008) 'Mobiles for development or poverty', Mobile Active, http://www.mobileactive08.org/node/954, accessed 4 June 2009.
13. Hari, J. (2008) 'How we fuel Africa's bloodiest war', *Independent*, 30 October, http://www.independent.co.uk/opinion/commentators/johann-hari/johann-hari-how-we-fuel-africas-bloodiest-war-978461.html, accessed 18 June 2009.
14. Farouk, F. (2008) 'UmNyango – a survey of the potential of the short messaging service: exteral evalutation of the Fahamu Umnyango project'.
15. Hash (2007) 'Why the internet matters in Africa', White African, http://whiteafrican.com/2007/12/31/why-the-internet-matters-in-africa/, accessed 28 September 2009.

16. Hersman, E. 'Mashups and activism', http://tinyurl.com/nnu2cx, accessed 23 June 2009. A mashup is a web application that takes two or more sets of data and combines them to create something of added value. The data types could be: maps (Google, Yahoo, NASA), images, video, audio, SMS data, Twitter (micro-blogging platform), personal information, indeed, almost any other type of data you can think of.

1

Economics and power within the African telecommunications industry

Nathan Eagle

Introduction

In the last decade we have witnessed the fastest technology adoption in human history. More than one billion mobile phones were sold during 2007, ten times as many as the number of personal computers sold that year, or one new phone for every six people on earth. In many developed countries the mobile phone penetration rate has exceeded 100 per cent of the population. However, mobile phones are now available to most people who earn more than US$5 a day, resulting in the fact that the majority of mobile phone subscribers today live in the developing world. As such, the mobile phone is really a developing world technology: people in the developing world represent the majority of users and it has had a far greater impact on their lives than on the lives of people in the West.

While mobile phones have fundamentally changed Africa in a variety of ways, the economic successes associated with the technology are multifaceted. A mobile phone service has been available in Africa for almost two decades but it is only relatively recently that mobile phone growth has truly taken off. In the first ten years that mobile phones were present in sub-Saharan Africa, they failed to make an impact due to factors such as high handset cost and service charges. However, recently, a combination of factors has led to dramatic increases in mobile phone subscribers. These factors include the reduction in the upfront costs of airtime and sim cards, as well as in handset prices, due to an onslaught of knock-off, 'grey-market' phones purchased from unauthorised distributors. Additionally, the regulatory landscape in individual countries played a large role: true competition starts when you get your fourth and fifth operator. What further helped was that the African market did not become a battle of the standards (TDMA/CDMA vs GSM) but adopted GSM in all markets, enabling even more competition and lower handset costs.

This chapter takes an overview of the economics of the telecommunications industry in Africa, details the economics associated with mobile operator equipment and licensing, discusses the limitations associated with mobile phone handsets sold in Africa, and provides some information about how foreign governments are using the telecommunications industry in Africa to increase their regional presence. The second section of this chapter focuses on the innovation that has recently emerged from an increasingly lucrative and competitive mobile phone market in East Africa, highlighting mobile payment services and the potential for USSD applications. It concludes with a discussion about opportunities for using the data generated by mobile phone operators for the public good, and takes a look at the associated privacy issues.

African mobile economics

When operators are asked why tariffs are so high, they inevitably cite the fact that they have to pay incredibly expensive GSM licensing fees. While recouping this massive investment is one obvious reason for pricing structure, another has to do simply with precedent. Although some operators in Africa (and throughout the world) are currently making incredible profits, in many other developing regions, such as Latin America, practically all the local small operators have disappeared, having been bought up by the giants such as TIM, Telefonica, America Movil (consolidation has not yet fully reached Africa, but will take place in the next five years). The reason for this is the massive upfront investment in licence, capex (costs associated with the acquisition of network equipment) and opex (operating expenses). Even in a small country in Africa, operators really cannot enter the game unless they have US$200 million to $1,000 million to spend. While for some of the lucky and proficient operators profit starts after year three or four, recouping this initial investment may take ten years. Despite this, the draw of these potential profits has lured many wealthy individuals and groups (generally from the Middle East, where the US stock market has even less appeal) to attempt to create their own mobile service providers – typically with limited success due to their level of experience with the market. It is also the unfortunate fact that many telecommunications regulatory committees within Africa are powerless to make the hard decisions against incumbent operators in favour of the public good.

East Africa: competition and profit margins

Competition and protectionism are two major reasons why GSM licences have increased in price across Africa. If a government owns half of the very lucrative, incumbent mobile operator, there is an incentive not to introduce additional competition to the market. Increasing the prices of GSM licences protects their investment, as well as increasing the money they receive should a competing operator decide the licence may indeed be worth the price. However, more operators also means more substantial bribes to government officials, and this may be why we are starting to see a dramatic increase in the number of operators across East Africa.

In Kenya, Safaricom, Kenya's largest mobile operator, will have over US$1 billion in revenue in 2009. Numbers like this have attracted a variety of western companies to join in a bidding war for a GSM licence in Kenya to compete. While the initial asking price for a GSM licence in Kenya was over US$100 million, the latest licence was sold to France Télécom (Orange) for approximately the same price as earlier licences (about US$55 million).

Uganda has been held as a model for how a country can go from having the second highest airtime rate in the world (after Turkey), to having a thriving mobile phone industry with some of the lowest airtime rates in East Africa. Instead of protecting its investments, the Ugandan government allowed virtually any mobile operator to purchase a GSM licence and begin a competing service within the country. By providing five licensed operators for a country with only five million subscribers, Uganda has created an extremely competitive telecommunications market resulting in dramatic reductions in the price of airtime across the country.

Equipment vendors: pay-to-play

Perhaps less visible to the public, but almost equally large and expanding as rapidly as the mobile operator businesses, is the industry of companies selling equipment to the mobile phone operators. Equipment vendors such as Huawei and ZTE have had exponential growth in terms of volume, but equipment prices have been declining almost as rapidly at approximately 20 per cent per year. Despite shrinking margins, the competitive landscape is incredibly crowded and none of the vendors are exiting. Competition is so tight that vendors are beginning to finance not only their own equipment but also the operators' licences and operating costs for several years just to get a contact. The situation is compounded by subsidised equipment from China, priced at 30 to 50 per cent lower than anything else on the market. Financing of the telecommunications industry by governments such as China is a strategic move to increase regional presence, similar to mobile operators in East Africa being funded by the Libyan government.

Additionally, because it has become the norm to give away the hardware and to charge operators a usage fee, this agreement with equipment vendors prevents operators from being able to experiment with new products and services because the fees from the vendors are simply too high. For example, operators like MTN Rwanda are attempting to prototype novel USSD (see p. 8) applications, yet to actually try out anything, the operators are required to pay the equipment vendor US$20,000 per potential application. This type of constraint has hampered innovation to such a degree that operators are forced to purchase redundant USSD gateways from other vendors to develop and launch novel and innovative services.

Handset vendors: mobile web conundrum

Most phones that are designed for and marketed to the African market today are not data enabled. These phones have no browser nor any ability to function as a traditional data device; their legacy (the average life span of a phone in Africa is many times that of its western counterpart) will affect mobile internet usage in these regions throughout the next decade. Furthermore, in much of rural Africa, fewer than one in ten phones can support the traditional 'mobile web' experience, and it is probably closer to one in one thousand phones that have ever successfully connected to the internet. Most of the phones in rural villages were originally manufactured before 2003.

The local mobile operators should take some blame for the lack of penetration of the mobile web as well – many simply do not have the equipment or expertise to roll out a data network on top of their rapidly expanding GSM network.[1] Additionally, operators, concerned about cannibalising their SMS revenues, are de-incentivised to push GPRS-enabled services.

The phones that sell in the African markets have the least number of frills beyond an LED flashlight partially due to economics – people value price above almost all other potential features. However, as the marginal cost for adding more sophisticated (e.g. mobile web) features continues to decrease, this cycle will eventually end – hopefully sooner rather than later.

Government: telco diplomacy

The telecommunications industry has presented an opportunity for foreign governments to increase their presence in sub-Saharan Africa. Under the guise of companies such as ZTE and Huawei, the Chinese government can take over a country's entire telecommunications industry, as in Ethiopia. A government-run operator such as the Ethiopian Telecommunications Corporation (ETC) coupled with a monopoly equipment vendor leads to a pricing structure with airtime rates comparable to those in Africa over a decade ago. Additionally, because the government has more incentive to stay in power than to turn a profit, communication channels such as SMS and GPRS have been made illegal until very recently (making it that much harder to teach SMS application development at the local universities). More worryingly, there are engineers currently held in prison, without being charged, presumably for conducting engineering quality assessments of the Chinese equipment that turned out not to be positive. An

Ethiopian telecommunications professor was recently forced to flee the country with his family when his similar conclusion about the equipment was made public.

China is not the only government attempting to gain influence in sub-Saharan Africa through the telecommunications industry. Libya, vying to further strengthen its prominent position within the African Union, has been putting substantial resources across East Africa – buying GSM licences and funding operators that, to date, have been struggling with commercial profitability. Operators funded by the Middle Eastern backers (typically from Saudi Arabia and UAE), however, are able to take a long perspective because they have access to significant excess capital, which allows them to be extremely aggressive with airtime pricing and gaining additional subscribers.

Innovation leap-frog

While much of the previous section focused on the negative realities associated with the African telecommunications industry, the recent increase in both revenue and competition has spurred a variety of truly innovative applications. Additionally, industries that have remained unchanged for decades, ranging from water to electricity companies, are beginning to look to mobile phones as a method of changing their business model. In order to differentiate themselves in an increasingly competitive market, operators are starting to deploy unprecedented services.

M-PESA

One such service is Safaricom's M-PESA which enables subscribers to send and receive money through their mobile phones. Money can be sent and redeemed at any post office or one of the thousands of M-PESA agents throughout Kenya. Not only is this service extremely popular for remittances (within the service's first year, Safaricom became the largest bank in East Africa), but services such as M-PESA provide the foundation for an entirely new suite of applications that can leverage this mobile payment system. A water pump company in Nairobi, for example, has sold water pumps in rural Kenya for many years, but recently changed their business model away from hardware sales, and instead they sell water 'vending machines'. Essentially this company attached a phone and a solar panel to their water pump and now, instead of paying for the pump with upfront capital, the villagers get the pump for free and M-PESA small amounts of money to the pump in exchange for water.

txteagle

Another service that leverages the M-PESA back-end is txteagle. txteagle enables mobile phone subscribers to earn small amounts of money by completing tasks for companies who pay them in either airtime or M-PESA. txteagle was originally launched with a set of translation tasks from Nokia and Google. By allowing people to receive money through the mobile phone, Safaricom has created another revenue stream not only for themselves (the operator charges transactional fees for the use of M-PESA), but also for their subscribers.

SMSMedia and ElectroGaz

In many African countries, electricity is prepaid. For example, in Rwanda, until recently, individuals had to travel to the capital and wait in line at the national electricity company, ElectroGaz, to top-up their accounts. This posed a dilemma: in a cash-strapped economy, most people could not afford to outlay a significant amount of capital, yet they did not have the time to go into town and wait in line every few days and keep their electricity account topped up to prevent their service being automatically shut off. Jeff Gasana at SMSMedia in Kigali recognised that just as prepaid airtime can be sold by scratch-card dealers, so could prepaid electricity. SMSMedia partnered with ElectroGaz and printed their own electricity scratch-cards. Within a year of launching this service, over 30 per cent of electricity users in Rwanda were using their mobile phones to buy electricity using SMSMedia's system.

The USSD potential

Much of the western world is unaware of the USSD protocol, but it is typically used almost as much as SMS. As opposed to SMS, USSD is a not a store-and-forward protocol, but rather is sessions based (a difference similar to that between email and telnet). Typically USSD is the method for prepaid subscribers to check their balance and top-up their account. Initiating a USSD session is typically done by entering the following numbers \emph{*shortcode\#command\#} and pressing send.

While deploying a USSD service typically requires collaboration with an operator, it is possible for a single operator to deploy a USSD service to virtually all of the four billion GSM mobile phones in use today. The implications of this potential are significant: because most operators keep USSD ports open for roaming traffic, global services can be deployed to most of the subscribers in Africa without the subscribers incurring any cost, irrespective of their mobile phone operator. Although this has been verified with application prototypes, there have yet to be any mainstream applications that take advantage of this fact.

Call data records for public good

This section looks at the potential of large-scale mobile phone data sets currently being generated in Africa. Such analytics could provide a better understanding of social relationships and information flows in disadvantaged societies, as well as guiding and monitoring information and communication technology for development (ICT-D) interventions and public policy and giving insight into population responses to crises. We are beginning to explore how machine learning and inference could help us understand human mobility patterns, yielding real-time estimates of the progression of disease outbreaks, for example, and guiding public health interventions.

Every one of the approximately 300 million mobile phones in Africa today has continuous access to information about an individual's social behaviour, including communication (phone calls and SMS), movement (cellular towers associated with the phone) and even financial transactions (airtime/money transfers, scratch-cards and new service purchases). The nature of mobile phones makes them an ideal vehicle to study both individuals and societies: people habitually carry a mobile phone with them and use it as a medium through which to do much of their communication. Mobile phones are inconspicuous, typically carried by the majority of a population, and have passive sensing capabilities that make them an important tool to study human populations. The recent ubiquity of mobile phones means that most people today already have the habit of keeping a charged behavioural sensor with them at all times. Every mobile phone in Africa also creates logs of communication and movement patterns that are stored within mobile phone service-provider databases throughout the continent.

While obtaining access to these operator databases is not a trivial process for researchers, today's mobile phone service providers occasionally allow limited access to the data they log about their subscribers' behaviour.[2, 3, 4] This data, typically referred to as call data records (CDR), consists of all communication events (phone calls and text messages) as well as the cellular tower that enabled the communication to occur. Beyond documentation of voice and text-message communication and location estimates based on cellular towers, occasionally mobile operators have additional data about their subscribers, including demographic information, socio-economic status, prepaid scratch card denominations, airtime sharing and transfers, and additional product adoption data.

It is important to emphasise the typical constraint on CDR: location of a phone is only logged if it is actively being used to communicate. While a mobile phone continuously monitors signals from proximate cellular towers, it typically does not, due to power constraints, continuously send back similar signals alerting the nearby towers of its particular location.[5]

Artificial intelligence for development (AI-D)

There has been great interest in ICT-D over the last several years. The work is diverse and extends from information technology that provides infrastructure for micropayments to techniques for monitoring and enhancing the cultivation of crops. While efforts in ICT-D have been interdisciplinary, ICT-D has largely overlooked opportunities for harnessing machine learning and reasoning to create new kinds of services, and to serve a role in analyses of data that may provide insights about socio-economic development for disadvantaged populations. The unprecedented volume of mobile phone data currently being generated in Africa on movement, communication and financial transactions provides new opportunities for applying artificial intelligence methods to development efforts in a sub-domain we are calling artificial intelligence for development (AI-D).

Absence of longitudinal data

Most data used for social research (including that generated by mobile phones) tends to provide static, behavioural snapshots. However, longitudinal data (time-series data logged over an extended duration) is essential to discriminating between cause and effect in behaviour data. For example, in some ongoing research on the effect cities have on their inhabitants' social networks, we can find that individuals who live in cities tend to have different types of social networks from those who live in rural areas, as hypothesised in previous studies.[6] However, a legitimate critique of this result is that the original question has gone unanswered. With the current snapshot data, we cannot tell whether the city attracts individuals who already have a signature social network, or whether indeed the city itself influences the network of its inhabitants. To obtain a better answer to this question it is necessary to have longitudinal data. Now that we have over three years of data on every mobile phone subscriber in the country, we can identify individuals who live in rural areas during year one, and then move to urban areas in year two. By comparing their 'before and after' social networks we can get a better idea of the effect of the city. Indeed with several years of data, we can also learn whether these individuals maintain these new relationships created in the urban area if they move back to their rural home.

Mobility patterns

The recent analysis of data from mobile phone service providers has given researchers increased insights into human movement patterns. While some researchers take issue with labelling these insights as 'universal laws of human movement', it is clear that through the analysis of cellular tower location data from hundreds of thousands of people, it is finally possible to quantify some of the more fundamental rules of human motion. As additional researchers replicate these findings using data from other countries and cultures, we will be even closer to quantifying the laws governing the physics of society.

Urban studies

The analysis of cellular tower data not only provides insight into human movement patterns, but also sheds some light on how individuals use the urban infrastructure within a city. Calabrese and Ratti have demonstrated the possibility of using mobile phones for urban analysis: to quantify the dynamics of complex urban activities.[7] As alluded to in the previous section, we are also hoping to use our Rwandan data to learn more about the effect cities have on their inhabitants' social networks.

Social network diversity

In our analysis of communication logs from the UK, individuals who communicate with a variety of different people have a greater socio-economic status. While it is not possible to establish causality between this behaviour and socio-economic status, there is a significant ($R = -0.75$, $p < .001$) correlation between a region's communication diversity and its index of deprivation (the metric for socio-economic status of the UK Civil Service). It certainly seems plausible that some cultures encourage interactions with others while other groups prefer to remain insular. In the US the type of culture encouraging interactions was shown to be associated with business school students and in the UK this culture appears to be associated with individuals of higher socio-economic status. The question whether this result is universal across countries is actively being pursued.

Economic indicators: scratch-card denominations

The vast majority of subscribers in Africa are on prepaid plans which necessitate the periodic purchase of airtime scratch cards, a ubiquitous commodity readily available in both the urban and rural areas of virtually every African country. Scratch cards are sold in a variety of denominations ranging from the equivalent of US$0.25 to US$20. We postulate that given a fixed call volume, individuals who purchase higher-denomination cards are more economically advantaged than individuals who purchase the same total amount of airtime incrementally using many, smaller-denomination scratch cards. We have recently made progress towards validating this hypothesis by showing that individuals living in the capital city use card denominations that are almost twice as much as the card denominations used within rural regions of the county, mapping well to government census data about socio-economic status levels within the capital, urban and rural regions of this particular African country.

Disease monitoring

An additional application area for CDR is to model the dissemination of a contagion, whether it is an airborne pathogen or the diffusion of a parasite such as malaria. The majority of epidemiological models assume that the host population is well mixed, such that the probability of infection is equal for all. Social network structures are clearly not always well mixed, however, and the complexities of people's interactions and movements may have profound implications for the interpretation of epidemiological models and clinical data. The accurate quantification of a population's movement and contacts, and therefore the associated variability in the probability of infection, is clearly of great importance. While hypothetical models are valuable for understanding the kind of effect different social network structures would have on disease spread, CDR can provide a much more realistic interpretation of human social network dynamics. With detailed data on mixing parameters (which quantify the proximity patterns of groups of people in a society) within unstudied populations in Africa and the developing world, epidemiologists will be armed with more information to make predictions about an area's vulnerability to the next SARS, or better decisions about the placement of malaria eradication resources, as well as having greater insight into preventing future epidemics.

Implementation challenges of CDR

Mobile phone service providers already have a wealth of movement and communication information in their call data records. While there are obvious benefits to using existing CDR for social research, often the benefits are outweighed by the issues and limitations associated with these types of data. The first obstacle is simply obtaining access to CDR data. Even upon agreement from a service provider, we have found that it takes months for legal documents to be written and signed before such a data-sharing agreement can be finalised.

Additionally, one of the major limitations with data from mobile phone service providers is the fact that it contains communication events and cellular tower location information only from when the phone is being used to make or receive a call or text message. This means that for almost all the time, the phone's location is unknown. Besides the limitations associated with the behavioural data that is automatically generated, collecting survey data about the subscribers is typically a time-intensive and expensive procedure. And many service providers, particularly in the developing world, have no demographic information about any of their subscribers. However, some providers do collect fairly detailed information about demographics including gender, pay scale, and address.

While mobile phone service providers have a financial incentive to maintain the quality of their data for billing purposes, the sheer magnitude of this type of data can be incredibly daunting to any researcher. For our analysis of data from the UK involving over 100 million phone numbers, we needed to obtain a computer with eight terabytes of extremely fast access drives (RAID 10), 64 gigabytes of memory and eight processors. Even with a machine such as this, we were unable to hold the full social network in memory, which makes calculating particular network metrics, such as distance, all the more challenging. Custom software needs to be written for the CDR analysis, which is in a continual state of development.

Privacy implications for rights activists

There are substantial privacy implications associated with using the data that is automatically generated by the hundreds of millions of mobile phone subscribers in Africa. While the dozens of operators across the continent are already continuously logging every mobile phone user's communication behaviour as well as location from nearby cell towers, most of the 300 million African subscribers being tracked are not cognisant of it.

With a democratic and open society, the argument can be plausibly made that privacy concerns can be balanced by the various benefits of convenience. However, benevolent governments are not guaranteed indefinitely (nor are they particularly common in Africa), and putting in place a vast system for information gathering has some rather disturbing consequences with a less than benevolent government. It is interesting to note that there are over 100 million people living in a variety of repressive African regimes who daily carry what is essentially an always-on surveillance device. It is still unclear what governments will begin to do with this type of data, and what kind of backlash it will have on activism.

Already some governments, such as that of Ethiopia, have banned text messaging because it was a communication medium used to organise political demonstrations. While this ban was recently repealed, the Ethiopian government's rationale for allowing text messaging once again is very much uncertain. It is quite possible that these governments now view the surveillance capabilities of the communication medium as offsetting its potential for generating political unrest.

A pervasive information-gathering system could be put to nefarious uses, especially in the hands of an unscrupulous government. But while we could (and perhaps should) raise attention to those obvious dangers, at the end of the day having a centralised cellular infrastructure implicitly creates such an information-gathering system. And if the system exists, why not use it for public service applications? Currently, society's use for this new type of data from mobile phones is to show that an individual has been at the scene of a crime. If we, as a society, agree that it is acceptable to use this data against an individual, then using it to better support the individual does not appear so controversial.

There does not appear to be a conclusive answer to the question about whether or not the privacy concerns surrounding mobile phones outweigh their potential benefits. The case that this chapter has tried to make is that assuming we do live in a society (benevolent or not) that does have a ubiquitous cellular infrastructure, it makes sense to start thinking about beneficial ways we (as engineers/designers/politicians/scientists and so on) can start using the resultant data.

While some may argue that this type of pervasive behavioural data should not be collected, it is a fact of life in the 21st century – the data discussed here will continue to be aggregated by the hundreds of mobile phone service providers throughout the world, whether or not it is shared with researchers. Therefore, while academics must remain cognisant of the privacy issues surrounding the analysis of personal information, society has much to gain from these studies and their potential for use in solving social problems ranging from disease outbreaks to urban planning. To achieve these goals, new tools will be needed to grapple with data sets that are many orders of magnitude larger than have previously existed.

Notes

1. It took the author over ten days of phone calls with his local Kenyan operator to get his account activated for their new EDGE network. Many people typically give up after the first couple of hours of configuration – and that's assuming they actually have the right phone.
2. Eagle, N. (2008) 'Behavioral inference across cultures: using telephones as a cultural lens', *IEEE Intelligent Systems*, vol. 23, no. 4, pp. 62–4.
3. Gonzalez, M., Hidalgo, C. and Barabasi, L.A. (2008) 'Understanding individual human mobility patterns', *Nature*, vol. 453, pp. 779–82.
4. Onnela, J., Saramaki, J., Hyvonen, J., Szabo, G., Lazer, D., Kaski, K., Kertesz, J. and Barabasi, A.L. (2007) 'Structure and tie strengths in mobile communication networks', *Proceedings of the National Academy of Sciences*, vol. 104, pp. 7332–6.
5. Operators can 'ping' a phone to have it report back to a nearby tower, however this requires additional power from the phone and therefore typically is impractical for continuous location tracking.
6. Fischer, C. (1982) *To Dwell Among Friends: Personal Networks in Town and City*, Chicago, Il, University of Chicago Press.
7. Calabrese, F. and Ratti, C. (2006) 'Real time Rome', *Networks and Communication Studies – Official Journal of the IGU's Geography of Information Society Commission*, vol. 20, no. 3, pp. 247–58.

Acknowledgments

This work is in large part due to interviews with individuals within Africa's telecommunications industry.

2

Mobile activism in Africa: future trends and software developments

Christian Kreutz

Introduction

The mobile phone will be a strategic tool for communication, collaboration, coordination and collective action with four particularly promising trends for mobile activism. However, there remain many challenges. When one takes a look at the future of mobile phones in Africa, there seems to be a growing consensus about the impact that mobiles have close at hand. But as Nathan Eagle from EPROM says, 'People will work on their mobiles in Africa, we just don't know how yet'.[1] One main obstacle to foreseeing the future is the lack of statistics and the fact that there are not numerous examples of African mobile activism to look at. It is still simply a new phenomenon although the beginning of mobile activism dates back to 2001 when, with the help of mobile phones, an organised protest wave in the Philippines ended the presidency of Jose Estrada.[2] Mobile phones are already within the reach of most people in Africa – according to the *2008 Africa Mobile Factbook*.[3] In 2012 only a minority of around 10 per cent will not have their own mobile phone. No other technology has ever had such a spread, not only in Africa, but also worldwide. Nowadays, mobile phones are used for all kinds of purposes and have a tremendous impact, and surely this will unleash even more opportunities. However, mobile activism is not necessarily different from other forms of activism, because it is, rather, a means to an end.

This chapter is an attempt to identify future trends for activism in the use of mobile phones. Africa is particularly interesting for analysing future trends because here the mobile has become the most decisive communication tool. The mobile phone combines all former media: to receive information, to document incidents with text, audio and video, to broadcast and publish content and to network with other mobile phone users.

However, in all fields of activism, such as advocacy, awareness, research, mobilisation and protest, mobiles can be a strategic tool for communication, collaboration, coordination and collective action.

Future trends

Looking at the existing potentials for mobile activism, it is striking to see how little mobile phones have been used in comparison to their overall distribution. Mobile phones can support various methods of activism with relatively little financial means compared to earlier times and other information and communication technology. There are already some free and open source software tools available to extend the basic features of mobiles. However, the adoption of the mobile as a key technology for activism is changing fast.[4] If one takes a look at the examples and different approaches of mobile activism, many potential developments can be identified. All these trends will rely not so much on technology, but much more on the activists' ideas for how to use mobile phones as a means of activism and on a critical mass of people participating. In addition, with the fast development of technology and its increasing adoption in recent years, the mobile phone will become an even more powerful tool in the next few years: 'A world in which nearly everyone owns a mobile linked into networks advanced enough to offer video and location-based services is years, not decades, away.'[5]

Here are some potential trends:

- Mobile participation through citizens' media
- Unprecedented local innovation around mobile tools and activism
- A powerful tool for monitoring and transparency
- Decentralised networking for coordination and mobilisation.

The first trend is about the use of mobile phones as a publishing and broadcasting tool. The mobile combines other mediums' feasibilities – potentially every user can be a recipient and publisher of news including text, audio and video. According to a report from Internews Europe,[6] since 2008 mobile phone access has, in many countries of the global South, surpassed the access to television. Media outlets such as Reuters offer services via mobile phones in developing countries.[7] Jasmine News[8] in Sri Lanka has over 100,000 subscribers to their SMS-based news alerts service.[9] But there is also a potential for a bottom–up approach through citizens' media. Citizens' media has flourished on the internet in recent years and mobile phones will become the future transmitter of media. Mobile citizens' media will establish new communication channels and links with other already existing forms of citizens' media.[10]

There have already been examples of convergence with other media such as radio, which is still very much the primary and most popular medium of communication in Africa. For example, radio stations often ask listeners to send feedback and requests by SMS. Ethan Zuckerman writes, 'Radios and mobile phones can serve as a broad-distribution, participatory media network with some of the same citizens' media dynamics of the internet, but accessible to a much wider and non-literate audience.'[11]

A good example of this trend is a project called Voices of Africa, in which mobile reporters across Africa use mobile phones to report on events and also send video interviews from an informal area, which are then published on the internet.[12] Mobiles can also be used to produce content, which can later be delivered to traditional media, such as the example of SW Radio Africa.[13] In these examples the mobile phone acts as a broadcasting tool which can potentially boost participation by also creating local content in different languages. Mobile phones will be used to get more people involved in writing about, documenting and sharing stories.[14] Mobile phones have already been applied as a key instrument for sending messages across borders in crisis situations. Often they are the only tool for activists in repressive regimes. One case is Egypt, where mobile phones are key to documenting human rights violations and to connecting instantly with human rights groups in emergency situations.[15] In Burma, short texts, photos or video footage were at some points the only evidence of protests. Particularly in remote areas, mobile phones are the only means to transmit information. Some countries already offer high bandwidth such as 3G, which could allow media activists to report live through video-equipped mobile phones to the internet and potentially to a global audience. Web services such as qik offer live video broadcasting options.[16] However, one of the key challenges is the risk of not having a local audience because access is too expensive and the necessary bandwidth is not available. Another area within this trend is the very active blogosphere in many African countries such as Nigeria, Kenya, Tanzania and South Africa. In the case of Tanzania, bloggers write in Kiswahili.[17] African bloggers from across the continent are at the forefront of this evolution and increasingly use their mobile phones for broadcasting, as happened during the 2007 elections in Kenya[18] (see Chapter 10) and the 2008 ones in Ghana.[19]

The second trend is local innovation around mobile activism. Since their widespread use in the global South, mobile phones have been used experimentally by activists for mobilisation and collective action, so a lot of new ideas for using mobile phones for activism have developed in Africa. These innovations will accelerate over the next few years as 'open source is democratising telephony as it already has internet publishing'.[20] Already, NGOs are benefiting in different ways from mobiles with the basic features of voice and SMS. According to a study by the United Nations Foundation, key benefits of mobile technology for all NGOs include time-savings (95 per cent), the ability to quickly mobilise or organise individuals (91 per cent), reaching audiences that were previously difficult or impossible to reach (74 per cent), the ability to transmit data more quickly and accurately (67 per cent), and the ability to gather data more quickly and accurately (59 per cent).[21]

Mobile phones offer many more possibilities for innovations that may not need much technical investment. For example, the tool FrontlineSMS (described in Chapter 3 of this book) only needs a computer and one mobile phone to become an SMS distribution channel from one to many users.[22] With few means, activists or NGOs can establish a decentralised communication network for information exchange or for coordination. FrontlineSMS is used to monitor elections, where people collect decentralised information from polling stations.[23] Mobile phones can be used in multiple settings and for multiple purposes[24] and it is up to the creativity of activists as to how they will use mobiles as an instrument to coordinate protests, mobilise for campaigns or do fundraising. So far, SMS and voice messages have been the main means of mobile usage. Applications with a speech interface, which allows people to interact with systems through their voices, have not been used very much. Exceptions include Question Box[25] and Freedom Fone from Kubatana in Zimbabwe (see Chapter 7), which provide a voice database where users can access news and public-interest information, via land or mobile, which is independent of the state-controlled media.[26] It is based on the free and open software called Asterisk, which is a toolkit for all kinds of telephony (voice) applications.[27]

As mobile phones have become a tool in the daily lives of most Africans, innovations are increasingly being developed around them.[28] Creativity and ingenuity are at play: through adapting or hacking mobile phones new uses are developed right where they are needed. One such initiative is EPROM, founded in Kenya, where students develop applications for low-cost and older models.[29]

There are high hopes for enabling internet connection around Africa to give activists new channels for communication and participation. There is a chance that grassroots activism could take more advantage of these tools and the rich data sources already available on the internet. Tino Kreutzer, in a study about mobile internet usage by low-income young South Africans, found that even with the constraints of costs, young people are increasingly eager to access the internet through their mobile phones. As Tino Kreutzer says, 'there is a high demand for good information'.[30] Although South Africa is not representative of the rest of Africa, there is a trend towards the mobile web. According to a report by Opera,[31] 'South Africa and Egypt lead the way for mobile web adoption, followed by Kenya and Nigeria'. Also, most of the traffic to the BBC mobile website comes from Africa.

The major interest is, according to Kreutzer, around music files or photos, but one-third of accessed pages in his research were from Google, to find information. Russell Southwood, a researcher from South Africa, highlights the benefit of valuable information for the poor and even their willingness to pay for it. He gives the example of an information service about prenatal care for poor people: 'There were 300 subscribers paying US$1.05 a month and by any description this is a health insurance scheme. As with using mobile phones, the poor will pay for what they really value'.[32]

However, on the whole the NGOs have not yet reacted to this growing interest and few mobile-based information services are offered by activists. If not text-based (SMS), a key requisite for this kind of access is GPRS-enabled phones, which most low-cost phones are not, yet – although GPRS is offered in many places throughout Africa.[33] The benefits of mobile-enabled activism will generate various experiments which can be complementary to existing forms of activism. Unlike the PC, the mobile phone will unleash a lot more innovation through its pervasiveness and accessibility.[34] Open operation systems allow the creation of various features needed for the local context and in the appropriate language.

Erik Hersman writes, 'It's becoming quite popular to create mobile products and services, but it's still fairly new'.[35] But there are African programmers who download software development kits to experiment with finding their own solutions for local needs. A key pre-requisite is that it is developed around the local context. Mark Davies from Tradenet said, 'It's all about understanding the agents of change and that's anthropology, not technology'.[36] Only then does it have the chance to grow, but in most cases it needs people: those who can get involved with new ideas or who identify a problem and the potential to tackle it through mobile-enabled activism; the programmer, who provides the solution; and lastly, the users, who know about it, know how to use it and want to use it. If that cooperation works well, new tools driven by free and open source software enable even small organisations to launch phone-based services at low costs.

The third trend is the use of mobile phones as a tool for monitoring and transparency. The following scenarios are promising in this regard:

- Building open information repositories through the participation of mobile users

- Establishing citizen monitoring systems to act as watchdogs
- Using advanced mobile features for analysis and independent research results.

All three developments overlap and have already been tested in some places, but there is an untapped potential to use the participation of mobile citizens. One example is Ushahidi, also described in this book (see Chapter 10), which collects different information from witnesses throughout a country or region.[37] This approach of engaging citizens for local information has the potential to be used in many other fields. Volunteers could send information to a central database about the quality of public services. Maps or detailed lists could be developed through participating citizens indicating how well schools or hospitals are taking care of them. Such coordinated efforts could lead not only to more transparency when monitoring elections, but it would also help collect grass-roots-driven statistics. This has happened, particularly in the area of HIV/AIDS,[38] and could be extended to many other areas. This would compensate for the lack of publicly available statistics and build a repository of valuable data independent of the state where public information is not available. Through the mobile, millions of users could contribute information to a central database. An application-programming interface (API) would then allow other activists to use this information for all advocacy campaigns.

Furthermore, the growing number of features of mobiles makes them a research tool that gives the user the capacity to analyse their environment. More and more citizens have a powerful mobile measurement instrument in their hands. A report from the United Nations Foundation documents an environmental monitoring project in Ghana where citizens 'use sensing-equipped mobile phones to monitor a range of environmental factors, from ambient air pollution to transportation and traffic patterns to noise pollution. Mobile sensing can paint a complex and dynamic portrait of the environment in which users are based.'[39] Nowadays, more and more people acquire mobile phones that have features such as videos, cameras, GPS or sensors (sooner or later), and other tools which allow analysis and documentation of the environment. Another example of the power of such activism for open repositories is the global initiative OpenStreetMap,[40] where volunteers worldwide help to create a digital map of the world freely available for everybody. The result is that for some cities in Africa OpenStreetMap has better maps than Google maps.[41] This could help activism around the issue of property rights and could create a lot more transparency if, for instance, these maps were extended with data from land title records. Mobile phones can become a key tool not only for collecting data in an unprecedented way, but also for using the results for advocacy and to mobilise activists across a country. The Collecting and Exchange of Local Agricultural Content project in Uganda is an excellent example of how this is applied in the local context. Farmers (see also Chapters 6 and 8) can document their knowledge about cultivation practices on different media and these are made available in a local repository.[42]

The fourth potential trend is towards user participation in decentralised networks for coordination and mobilisation. Engaging in a 'ubiquitous network' would bring benefits for activism such as coordination, mobilisation and collective action. 'It is not about mobile any more. This is a perfect example of the convergence of the social web with mobile telephony. The mobile lets you interact within a network in a highly contextual way,' says Teemu Arina.[43] Or, as anthropologist Jan Chipchase asks, 'So what does it mean when people's identity is mobile?'[44] Africa is not far away from that scenario when one looks at South Africa and Egypt. MXit in South Africa, a mobile social network application with more than five million members, lets people engage in their own community, independent of location and time.[45] MXit is a free instant-messaging software application that runs on GPRS/3G mobile phones with Java support and on PCs.[46] MXit is mainly used by young people and acts as a chat room, but messages are cheaper than regular SMS. One project in South Africa uses MXit for counselling services, where young people can address burning questions on topics such as violence or sexuality and receive answers.[47] Although it is a chat tool, it shows the potential for peer-to-peer networking, where activists can be connected with each other everywhere. Different from SMS campaigns, which are vertical and often do not allow feedback, projects like MXit could create networks built around causes.

Some activists have developed an application on Android, an

open source system introduced by Google, where you can find networks through your mobile for different causes, such as the environment, and interact solely with your mobile phone.[48] In African countries with a higher convergence of media, there are signs of mobiles and the internet combining to enable networks for protests. Because we are witnessing new forms of activism, which are not necessarily driven by NGOs or the 'ad-hoc networks' of any particular groups, those who are mobilised through SMS or network applications can initiate protests in spontaneous flash mobs.[49] These patterns can be seen in spontaneous protest groups on Facebook, where, in the case of Egypt in spring 2008, up to 70,000 people joined a group to support strikes in factories around the Nile delta.[50] About 800,000 Egyptians are members of the social network Facebook, and in a not so distant future they will expand their networks, with mobile phones interacting from everywhere.[51] A lot of these campaigns have happened in recent years through the exchange of SMS, where it is not necessarily a group or organisation that is the initiator, but an individual, who starts by sending a complaint to friends.

Another good example of this kind of network effect is Twitter, a web-based social network tool, which members use to communicate through short messages via the web and over mobile phones.[52] A simple SMS sent from anywhere is published on the web and can inform peers everywhere else. Egyptian activists have used this tool to spread information about their imprisonment or emergencies virtually within minutes.[53] The messages via mobile phone are published on Twitter, where followers of the activists can read them and spread the news within their own networks. In some cases, within a short time, counteractions can be launched and new campaigns set up within hours of the detention of the activists.

Challenges

Are we witnessing a shift towards multiple forms of mobile activism? Surely not, in the sense that mobile phones are merely an instrument, completely reliant on the engagement of people and the extent to which the phones are embedded into an existing activism strategy. The best application has no effect without a critical mass of participation or engagement. Ken Banks writes, 'One of the biggest challenges in the social mobile space is outreach and promotion, and we need to take advantage of every opportunity to get news on available solutions – and successful deployments – right down to the grassroots.'[54] As with every other instrument in the toolbox of an activist, there is also a list of its limitations at different levels. The most obvious constraints are the high costs of calls and SMS when participating in any of these scenarios. One result is the culture around 'beeping' – mobile users send messages simply using the frequency of rings to an agreed code in order to save money.[55]

Another obstacle is the lack of skills – a certain media competency is indispensable to master all the features of a mobile and fully participate in mobile activism. Smart phones, with many additional features, are beyond the reach of most Africans due to their high cost. The most widely dispersed mobile phones, namely the low cost ones, rarely offer all the features described above. Not only is data access a constraint, but there are also issues of privacy because mobiles are often shared or lent, for example, when there is a village phone.

A major problem is still the disparities between urban and rural areas. Not only is the urban population often wealthier, their urban location also gives them better access to information whereas rural areas are more cut off. In many ways, when it comes to activism, they are often only recipients of messages such as SMS campaigns.[56] However, a major part of mobile communication is happening locally and could be much better used if prices were not so high and the infrastructure was better. Mobile providers often have little economic interest in offering access to rural areas. Therefore, a major challenge for mobile activism is how to bring the infrastructure to areas where mobile providers are unwilling to invest. Ian Howard argues, 'The development of autonomous infrastructure is still required in order to meet the needs of rural communities ... These new mobile-phone infrastructures are largely poised as oligopolies, protected from the threat of new entrants by high licensing fees and reserved frequency allotments.'[57]

There are overall obstacles, such as regulatory frameworks and government requirements, which can hinder the growth of mobile phones or limit the mobile controlling and blocking services. For example, in Ethiopia SMS was blocked,[58] and in Kenya and Nigeria it is no longer permitted to purchase a mobile phone anonymously. Mobile phone networks can be monitored by mobile providers and authoritarian governments. For example, every mobile phone that is in use can be tracked to its location.

There are quite a lot of developments all around the world of freely available mobile applications such as FrontlineSMS, Mesh4x,[59] Open Rosa[60] and many more, but the landscape of developers and participating organisations is quite fragmented. Many applications are works in progress and are not necessarily easily used without a level of expertise that is not widely available among activist groups or NGOs. Also, applications so far need to be SMS-based in order to reach the majority of people. Most low cost mobiles are not built to include, for example, data exchange, which is essential for recently developed applications. So there is a bit of a chicken and egg dilemma – not enough useful applications for social issues are developed because too few people can access these applications, but the necessary mobile hardware is not included in the low cost mobile phones. Often, there is simply not a critical mass of potential users, which means it is not worth investing in or building strategies for activism around mobile phones. On top of that, most mobile providers treat their mobile networks as a walled garden, where access to extended services or software is only possible through their channels.[61]

Finally, one has to look carefully at whether the mobile really delivers added value, or whether other means benefit the cause better. A theatre group might have more impact on the issue of HIV/AIDS than an SMS campaign. There is a risk that the mobile phone might replace old forms of activism that enabled more people to participate and might, in the local context, be more appropriate. The new channels have a lot of potential, but they cannot replace traditional forms of activism and can only act as transmitters and amplifiers. Whatever new potential mobile activism harnesses, like all other activism, it needs to address one essential challenge: the lack of participation.

Notes

1. Goldstein (2008) 'People will work on their mobiles in Africa, we just don't know how yet', http://inanafricanminute.blogspot.com/2008_09_01_archive. html, accessed 22 February 2009.
2. Rheingold, H. (2003) *Smart Mobs: The Next Social Revolution*, New York, Basic Books.
3. http://www.africantelecomsnews.com/Factbook_form.html, accessed 22 February 2009.
4. Kinkade, S. and Verclas, K. (2008) *Wireless Technology for Social Change: Trends in NGO Mobile Use*, Washington DC and Berkshire, UK, UN Foundation-Vodafone Group Foundation, http://www.unfoundation.org/ press-centre/publications/wireless-technology-for-social-change.html, accessed 24 February 2009.
5. West, J. (2008) 'The promise of ubiquity', Paris, Internews Network, http:// www.internews.fr/spip.php?article459, accessed 14 April 2009.
6. Ibid.
7. Roy, V. C. (2008) 'Reuters expands mobile info service to Punjab', http:// www.business-standard.com/india/storypage.php?autono=337980, accessed 16 July 2009.
8. *JNW News*, http://www.jasminenews.com/about-jnw, accessed 14 April 2009.
9. West, J. (2008).
10. Ibid.
11. Zuckerman, E. (2007) 'Mobile phones and social activism', http://www. techsoup.org/learningcentre/hardware/page7216.cfm, accessed 24 February 2009.
12. Nyirubugara, O. (2007) 'Mobile reporters in Africa', http://www. africanews.com/site/page/voicesofafrica, accessed 22 February 2009.
13. Lipsett, A. (2008) 'Brilliant way to get news to Zimbabwe', *Guardian*, 14 November, http://www.guardian.co.uk/education/2008/nov/14/mediastudi escommunicationsandlibrarianship-internationalstudents, accessed 22 February 2009.
14. Share Ideas http://www.shareideas.org/index.php/News:Collaborative_ Learning_Across_Continents, accessed 24 February 2009.
15. Simon, M. (2008) 'Student "Twitters" his way out of Egyptian jail', *CNN* http://www.cnn.com/2008/TECH/04/25/twitter.buck/index.html, accessed 24 February 2009.
16. qik, 'Share live video from your phone!', http://qik.com/, accessed 24 February 2009.
17. Tungaraza, N. (2007) 'Blogging for social change', http:// globalvoicesonline.org/2007/07/07/blogging-for-social-change-interview-with-jeff-msangi/, accessed 24 February 2009.
18. Were, D. (2007) 'Election07', http://www.mentalacrobatics.com/think/ archives/category/africa/kenya/election07, accessed 24 February 2009.
19. Serra, E.V. (2008) 'Twittering the Ghanaian elections', http:// globalvoicesonline.org/2008/12/08/twittering-the-ghanaian-elections/,

accessed 24 February 2009.

20. West, J. (2008).

21. Kinkade, S. and Verclas, K. (2008).

22. FrontlineSMS (2009), http://www.frontlinesms.com/what/, accessed 24 February 2009.

23. Banks, K. (2007) 'The Nigerian elections: a short history of FrontlineSMS', Pambazuka News, http://www.pambazuka.org/en/category/comment/41128, accessed 24 February 2009.

24. Nesbit, J. (2009) 'Why FrontlineSMS fits', http://mobilesinmalawi.blogspot.com/2009/01/why-frontlinesms-fits.html, accessed 19 September 2009.

25. Doctorow, C. (2008) 'Question Box: the internet for remote places, no literacy or keyboards required', http://www.boingboing.net/2008/03/04/question-box-the-int.html, accessed 24 February 2009.

26. 'Freedom Fone – Mobile Information Service' (2008) http://www.kubatana.net/html/ff/ff_cont.asp, accessed 22 February 2009.

27. Asterisk (2009) http://www.asterisk.org/, accessed 24 February 2009.

28. 'Ken Njoroge of Cellulant' (2009) http://whiteafrican.com/2008/09/22/5-examples-of-student-ingenuity-in-kenya/, accessed 24 February 2009.

29. EPROM (2009), http://eprom.mit.edu/, accessed 24 February 2009.

30. Kreutzer, T. (2009) 'Generation mobile: online and digital media usage on mobile phones among low-income urban youth in South Africa, complete survey results', http://tinokreutzer.org/mobile/MobileOnlineMedia-SurveyResults-2008.pdf, accessed 30 March 2009; Kreutzer, T. (2008) *Pilot Paper: Assessing Cell Phone Usage in a South African Township School*, Cape Town, University of Cape Town, Cape Town, http://www.tinokreutzer.com/mobile/, accessed 14 September 2009.

31. von Tetzchner, S. (2008) 'State of the mobile web', http://www.opera.com/smw/2008/09, accessed 11 March 2009.

32. Verclas, K. (2008) 'MobileActive08: critical analysis of mobiles for social change', http://mobileactive.org/mobileactive08-critical-analysis-field, conference report accessed 24 February 2009.

33. Williams (2008) 'Africa mobile factbook 2008', http://www.africantelecomsnews.com/Factbook_form.html, accessed 11 March 2009.

34. Banks, K. (2009) 'The "long tail" revisited' http://www.kiwanja.net/blog/2009/01/the-long-tail-revisited/, accessed 11 March 2009.

35. Hersman, E. (2008) 'Building mobile apps for Africa', http://whiteafrican.com/2008/12/16/building-mobile-apps-for-africa/, accessed 22 February 2009.

36. Verclas, K. (2008).

37. Ushahidi, http://www.ushahidi.com/, accessed 22 February 2009.

38. Wagh, M. 'Dialing for health in Africa' (2007) http://www.biotech360.com/biotechArticleDisplay.jsp?biotechArticleId=100006, accessed 24 February 2009.

39. Kinkade, S. and Verclas, K. (2008).

40. *OpenStreetMap*, http://www.openstreetmap.org/, accessed 14 April 2009.

41. Soden, R. (2009) 'OpenStreetMap gets the details in Africa', http://www.

developmentseed.org/blog/2009/jan/15/developing-countries-mapped-good-detail-open-street-map, accessed 22 February 2009.
42. CELAC, http://www.celac.or.ug/, accessed 11 March 2009.
43. Arina, T. (2008) 'How mobile is changing our society', http://tarina.
blogging.fi/2008/10/18/speaking-at-mobile-monday-amsterdam/, accessed 14 April 2009.
44. Chipchase, J. (2009) 'Talks: Jan Chipchase on our mobile phones', http://www.ted.com/index.php/talks/jan_chipchase_on_our_mobile_phones.html, accessed 14 April 2009.
45. MXit Lifestyle (2008) 'Next generation mobile instant messenger', http://www.mxit.co.za/web/index.htm, accessed 24 February 2009.
46. MXit Lifestyle (2009) 'Next generation mobile instant messenger', http://en.wikipedia.org/wiki/MXit, accessed 11 March 2009.
47. Peters, S. (2008) 'Using MXit to empower communities', http://www.bizcommunity.com/Article/196/78/29809.html, accessed 22 February 2009.
48. Marcondes, C., Martinello, M., Oliveira Santos Fabio Fabris, R., dePandolfi, B., Santos Coelho, R., Zagoto Mariano, L., Oliveira C. and Charra L. (2008) 'Join us! Mobile phone software management of enthusiast "flash mobs" interested in performing social tasks', Vitoria, Espirito Santo, Brazil, Federal University of Espirito Santo Computer Science Department, http://www.w3.org/2008/02/MS4D_WS/papers/joinus_v2.pdf, accessed 17 July 2009.
49. Wasik (2003) 'flash mob', http://en.wikipedia.org/wiki/Flash_mob, accessed 14 April 2009.
50. Shapiro, S. (2009) 'Revolution, Facebook-style', *New York Times*, 22 January, http://www.nytimes.com/2009/01/25/magazine/25bloggers-t.html?_r=1, accessed 24 February 2009.
51. Ibid.
52. 'Twitter', http://en.wikipedia.org/wiki/Twitter, accessed 11 March 2009.
53. Qantara.de (2007) 'Human rights in Egypt: fighting torture with mobile phones and weblogs', 16 March, http://www.qantara.de/webcom/show_article.php/_c-476/_nr-753/i.html, accessed 14 April 2009.
54. Banks, K. (2009) 'Social mobile: myths and misconceptions', http://www.kiwanja.net/blog/2009/02/social-mobile-myths-and-misconceptions/, accessed 11 March 2009.
55. Donner, J. (2007) 'The rules of beeping: exchanging messages via intentional "missed calls" on mobile phones', *Journal of Computer-Mediated Communication*, vol. 13, no. 1, article 1, http://jcmc.indiana.edu/vol13/issue1/donner.html, accessed 11 March 2009.
56. Ogada, J. (2008) 'Mobile and SMS for activism and advocacy', http://www.mobileactive08.org/node/966, accessed 11 March 2009.
57. *APCNews* (2008) 'Rural communication: Is there still a need for telecentres now that there are mobile phones?', 27 October, http://www.apc.org/en/news/wireless/all/rural-communication-there-still-need-telecentres-n, accessed 24 February 2009.
58. Grenville, M. (2007) 'News: Ethiopia restores SMS', 26 September, http://www.160characters.org/news.php?action=view&nid=2374, accessed 24 February 2009.

59. Mesh4x (2009) 'Mesh tools for multiple platforms', http://code.google.com/p/mesh4x/, accessed 14 April 2009.
60. Open Rosa, http://www.openrosa.org/, accessed 14 April 2009.
61. Hersman, E. (2008).

3

Social mobile: empowering the many or the few?

Ken Banks

Is the future of social mobile an empowered few, or an empowered many? Mobile tools in the hands of the masses present a great opportunity for NGO-led social change, but is that the future we're creating?

In *The White Man's Burden – Why the West's Efforts to Aid the Rest Have Done So Much Ill and So Little Good*,[1] William Easterly's[2] frustration at large-scale, top–down, bureaucracy-ridden development projects runs to an impressive 384 pages. While Easterly dedicates most of his book to markets, economics and the mechanics of international development itself, he talks little of information and communication technologies (ICT). The index carries no reference to 'computers', 'ICT' or even plain old 'technology'.

But there is an entry for 'cell phones'.

E. F. Schumacher,[3] a fellow economist and the man widely recognised as the father of the appropriate technology movement, spent a little more time in his books studying technology issues. His seminal 1973 book, *Small is Beautiful – The Study of Economics as if People Mattered*,[4] reacted to the imposition of alien development concepts on 'Third World' countries, and he warned early of the dangers and difficulties of advocating the same technological practices in entirely different societies and environments. Although his earlier work focused more on agri-technology and large-scale infrastructure projects (dam building was a favoured 'intervention' at the time), his theories could easily have been applied to ICT – as they were in later years.

Things have come a long way since 1973. For a start, many of us now have mobile phones, the most rapidly adopted technology in history. In what amounts to little more than the blink of an eye, mobiles have given us a glimpse of their potential to help us solve some of the most pressing problems of our time. With evidence mounting, I have one question: If mobiles truly are as revolutionary and empowering as they appear to be – particularly in the lives of some of the poorest members of society – then do we have a moral duty, in the ICT for Development (ICT-D)[5] community at least, to see that they fulfil that potential?

You see, I'm a little worried. If we draw parallels between the concerns of Easterly and Schumacher and apply them to the application of mobile phones as a tool for social and economic development, there's a danger that the development community may end up repeating the mistakes of the past. We have a golden opportunity here that we can't afford to miss.

But miss it we may. Since 2003 I've been working exclusively in the mobile space, and I've come to my own conclusions about where we need to be focusing more of our attention if we're to take advantage of the opportunity ahead of us. Don't get me wrong – we do need to be looking at the bigger picture – but there's not room at the top for all of us. I, for one, am more than happy to be working at the bottom. Not only do I find grassroots NGOs particularly lean and efficient (often with the scarcest of funding and resources), but they also tend to get less bogged down with procedure, politics and egos, and are often able to react far more quickly to changing environments than their larger counterparts. Being local, they also tend to understand their context better, and in activism terms they're more likely to be able to operate under the radar of dictatorial regimes, meaning they can often engage a local and national populace in ways where larger organisations might struggle.

In my experience, grassroots NGOs are generally small and extremely dedicated organisations, who run low-cost, high-impact interventions, work on local issues with relatively modest numbers of local people and are staffed by community members who have first-hand experience of the problems they're trying to solve. What they lack in tools, resources and funds they more than make up with a deep understanding of the local landscape – not just its geography, but also the language, culture and daily challenges of the people. It is these often unique insights which allow grassroots organisations more successfully to identify and adopt appropriate technology, tailored to the environments in which they work.

So, waving my grassroots NGO flag, I see a central problem of focus in the mobile applications space. Let me explain. If we take the 'long tail' concept first talked about by Chris Anderson[6] and apply it to the mobile space, we get something like you see in Figure 3.1. I call it 'Social mobile's long tail'.

What this illustrates is that our tendency to aim for sexy, large-scale, top–down, capital- and time-intensive mobile solutions simply results in the creation of tools which only the larger, more resource-rich NGOs are able to adopt and afford. Having worked with grassroots NGOs for over 15 years, I strongly believe that we need to seriously focus some of our attention on them to avoid developing our own NGO 'digital divide'. To do this we need to think about low-end, simple, appropriate mobile technology solutions which are easy to obtain, affordable, require as little technical expertise as possible and are easy to copy and replicate. This is something I write regularly about and it's a challenge I'm more than happy to throw down to the developer community.

Another key problem that we have emerges as a symptom of the first. Because larger international development agencies, by their very nature, tend to be preoccupied with the bigger issues, they often inadvertently neglect the simple, easier-to-fix problems (the 'low-hanging fruit' as some people like to call it). The Millennium Development Goals (MDGs)[7] are good examples of the kind of targets which are far easier to miss than hit: very high-level, national and international targets, which are generally attainable only through large, high-cost, highly scaled, top–down interventions.

In mobile terms, using the technology to enhance basic communications is a classic 'low-hanging fruit'. After all, that's what mobile phones do, and communication is fundamental to all NGO activities, particularly those working in the kinds of infrastructure-challenged environments often found in the developing world. Despite this, there are few tools available that take advantage of one of the most prolific mobile communication channels available to grassroots NGOs – the text message (or SMS).

Much of my own work with FrontlineSMS[8] has sought to solve this fundamental problem. FrontlineSMS is a piece of free software that turns a laptop (or desktop) computer, a mobile phone and a

Figure 3.1 Social mobile's long tail

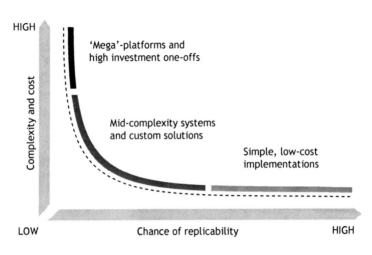

HIGH

'Mega'-platforms and
high investment one-offs

Complexity and cost

Mid-complexity systems
and custom solutions

Simple, low-cost
implementations

LOW   Chance of replicability   HIGH

Source : www.kiwanja.net

cable into a two-way group messaging centre. It is easy to install and use, and works using readily available hardware. In addition, once the software is downloaded and installed there is no need for the internet, which is crucial for organisations working in rural, communication-challenged environments, as many are.

Since its initial release in 2005, FrontlineSMS has been used by NGOs around the world for a wide range of activities. In Malawi, Josh Nesbit,[9] a laptop, one hundred recycled mobile phones and a copy of FrontlineSMS have helped revolutionise healthcare delivery to 250,000 rural Malawians. In other countries, where activities of international aid organisations may be challenged or restricted by oppressive, dictatorial regimes, grass-roots NGOs often manage to maintain operations and provide the only voice for the people. In Zimbabwe, Kubatana.net[10] (see Chapter 7) have been using FrontlineSMS extensively to engage a population starved not only of jobs, a meaningful currency and a functioning democracy, but also of news and information. In Afghanistan, an international NGO is using FrontlineSMS to provide 'security alerts to their staff and fieldworkers'.[11] The software is seen as a crucial tool in helping keep people safe in one of the world's most volatile environments. With a little will, what can be done in Zimbabwe and Afghanistan can be done anywhere that similar oppression exists.

In cases such as these – and there are many more – we need to stop simply talking about 'what works' and start to get 'what works' into the hands of the NGOs that need it the most. That's a challenge that I'm happy to throw down to the ICT-D community. There's only a certain amount of talking and critiquing we can, and should, do.

Part of the problem, however, is that there are numerous myths and misconceptions in the mobile space, many of which perpetuate the belief that developing high-end solutions is the best way forward. If we are to realise the true potential of mobile in the social mobile long tail, then the following myths and misconceptions need to be overcome.

'High-end is better than low-end'

First, one mobile tool should never be described as being better than the other – it's all about the context of the user. There is just as much a need for a US$1 million server-based, high-bandwidth, mobile-web solution as there is for a low-cost, SMS-only PC-based tool. Both are valid. Solutions are needed all the way along the 'long tail',[12] and users need a healthy applications ecosystem to dip into, whoever and wherever they may be. Generally speaking there is no such thing as a bad tool, just an inappropriate one.

'Don't bother if it doesn't scale'

Just because a particular solution won't ramp-up to run an international mobile campaign, or healthcare for an entire nation, does not make it irrelevant. Just as a long-tail solution is unlikely ever to run a high-end project, expensive and technically complex solutions would probably fail to downscale enough to run a small rural communications network. Let's not forget that a small deployment that helps just a dozen people is significant to those dozen people and their families.

'Centralised is better than distributed'

Not everything needs to run on a mega-server housed in the capital city, accessed through 'the cloud'.[13] Storing data and even running applications – remotely – might be wonderful technologically, but it's not so great if you have a patchy internet connection, if one at all. For most users centralised means 'remote', distributed 'local'.

'Big is beautiful'

Sadly, there is a general tendency to take a small-scale solution that works and then try to make a really big version of it. One large instance of a tool is not necessarily better than hundreds of smaller instances. If a small clinic finds a tool to help deliver healthcare more effectively to two hundred people, why not simply get the same tool into a thousand clinics? Scaling a tool changes its DNA, sometimes to such an extent that everything that was originally good about it is lost. Instead, replication is what's needed.

'Tools are sold as seen'

I would argue that everything we see in the social mobile applications ecosystem today is 'work in progress', and it is likely to remain that way for some time. The debate around the pros and cons of different tools needs to be a constructive one – based on a work-in-progress mentality – and one that positively feeds back into the development cycle.

'Collaborate or die'

Although collaboration is a wonderful concept, it doesn't come without its challenges – politics, ego and vested interests among them. There are moves to make the social mobile space more collaborative, but this is easier said than done. The next 12 months will determine whether or not true non-competitive collaboration is possible, and between who. The more meaningful collaborations will be organic, based on needs out in the field, not those formed out of convenience.

'Appropriate technology is poor people's technology'

This is a criticism often aimed more broadly at the appropriate technology movement, but locally powered, simple, low-tech-based responses should not be regarded as second best to their fancier, high-tech, 'western' cousins. A cheap, low-spec handset with five days' standby time is far more appropriate than an iPhone if you don't live anywhere near a mains outlet.

'No news is bad news'

For every headline-grabbing mobile project, there are hundreds, if not thousands, which never make the news. Progress and adoption of tools will be slow and gradual, and project case studies will bubble up to the surface over time. No single person in the mobile space has a handle on everything that's going on out there.

'Over-promotion is just hype'

Mobile tools will be adopted only when users get to hear about them, understand them and are given easy access to them. One of the biggest challenges in the social mobile space is outreach and promotion, and we need to take advantage of every opportunity to get news on available solutions, and successful deployments, right down to the grassroots. It is our moral duty to do this, as it is to help with the adoption of those tools that clearly work and improve people's lives.

'Competition is healthy'

In a commercial environment – yes – but saving or improving lives should never be competitive. If there's one thing that mobile-for-development practitioners can learn from the wider development and ICT-D community, it is this.

Even if we are able to make progress in these areas, there are many other issues and challenges to overcome – some technical, some cultural, others economic and geographical. The good news is that few are insurmountable, and we can remove many of them by simply empowering the very people we're seeking to help. The emergence of home-grown developer communities in an increasing number of African countries – Kenya, South Africa, Nigeria and Ghana, for example – presents the greatest opportunity yet to unlock the social-change potential of mobile technology. Small-scale, realistic, achievable, replicable, bottom–up development such as that championed by the likes of Easterly and Schumacher may hardly be revolutionary, but what would be is our acknowledgment of the mistakes of the past and a coordinated effort to help us avoid making them all over again.

I spent the best part of my university years critiquing the efforts of those who went before me. Countless others have done the same. Looking to the future, how favourably will the students and academics of tomorrow reflect on our efforts? If the next 30 years are not to read like the last then we need to rethink our approach, and rethink it now.

Notes

1. Easterly, W. (2006) *White Man's Burden*, Oxford, OUP, illustrated edition.
2. Wikipedia 'William Easterly', http://en.wikipedia.org/wiki/William_Easterly, accessed 18 May 2009.
3. Wikipedia, 'E. F. Schumacher', http://en.wikipedia.org/wiki/E._F._Schumacher, accessed 18 May 2009.
4. Schumacher, E.F. (1973) *Small is Beautiful*, Blond & Briggs.
5. Information & Communication Technology for Development.
6. Wikipedia, 'Chris Anderson', http://en.wikipedia.org/wiki/Chris_Anderson_(writer), accessed 18 May 2009.
7. Wikipedia, 'Millennium Development Goals', http://en.wikipedia.org/wiki/Millennium_Development_Goals, accessed 18 May 2009.
8. FrontlineSMS, http://www.frontlinesms.com/, accessed 18 May 2009.
9. Nesbit, J. 'Projects and perspectives on global health', http://www.jopsa.org/, accessed 18 May 2009.
10. Kubatana, http://www.kubatana.net, accessed 18 May 2009.
11. Banks, K. 'FrontlineSMS on the frontline', http://www.kiwanja.net/blog/2008/08/frontlinesms-on-the-frontline/, accessed 18 May 2009.
12. Banks, K. 'A glimpse into the social mobile long tail', http://www.kiwanja.net/blog/2009/01/a-glimpse-into-social-mobiles-long-tail/, accessed 18 May 2009.
13. Wikipedia 'Cloud computing', http://en.wikipedia.org/wiki/Cloud_computing, accessed 18 May 2009.

4

Mobiles in-a-box: developing a toolkit with grassroots human rights advocates

Tanya Notley and Becky Faith

Born out of change

The way information is created, accessed, reviewed, contested and used to drive social change has been changing rapidly over the past five years. The rise of Web 2.0 technology and the increasing popularity of user-level tools and services such as YouTube, Flickr and Blip.tv, alongside other non-commercial alternatives such the Witness Hub, EngageMedia and World Social Forum TV, have created greater opportunities for dynamic information sharing, content collaboration and self-publishing. The potential for these tools and services to contribute to human rights advocacy work has increased considerably as new ICT has become cheaper and more accessible to people living in marginalised communities, as well as progressively more interlaced: mobile phones feed into websites, websites become interactive radio stations, and the offline and online world increasingly interconnect. But just as emerging technology brings new opportunities, it also presents new challenges by introducing new methods for suppression, censorship and breaches of privacy. Evolving technology also creates a 'moving target', and the gap between people who have low-cost and high-quality broadband internet and multimedia mobile access in the global North with those who have expensive basic mobiles and infrequent or slow internet connectivity in the global South remains large.

In 2003 Tactical Technology Collective was born out of this

evolving and unequal ICT global landscape. The founders of Tactical Tech were inspired by the work of human rights advocates, and motivated by a belief that a great opportunity existed for technology to make a contribution towards this work. Importantly, they were involved in and influenced by the growth of the free and open source software and e-rider[1] movements, both of which provided evidence of the power of self-organised, distributed, open technology structures to design tools and services that meet local needs. However, the Tactical Tech founders also recognised that while open source and human rights advocates tended to be philosophically aligned, they did not interact as much as they ought to. Tactical Tech was established to help build bridges between the innovative activities these two movements were involved in.

When Tactical Tech first began its work in 2003, there were a number of barriers preventing human rights advocates from exploiting ICT. For example, many advocates were unaware of the full range of possibilities for using ICT effectively in their work, while others lacked the ability to choose the right tools or the expertise to put them to use. Added to this were all kinds of technological, economic, legal, social and political barriers – ranging from exorbitant call charges and limited base stations in non-urban areas to prohibitive laws and policies that banned or heavily monitored mobile services such as text messaging – that were acting to prevent widespread, equally distributed ICT uptake and use. Tactical Tech also knew that process mattered: no matter what technology is ultimately chosen, it needs to be thoughtfully integrated into advocacy work – not merely tagged on at the end of a process.

To address these issues, rather than establish a centralised pool of staff to implement new projects, the Tactical Tech founders built a strong network of affiliations with like-minded human rights advocates and technologists living on every continent: programmers, graphic designers, social activists, open source advocates and media producers. Tactical Tech now functions as a distributed, networked organisation, meeting from time to time when it's possible, gathering in two 'hubs' in the UK and India, but mostly communicating, planning, strategising, debating, creating and organising using the ICT they believe can support positive social change. Rather than devising projects for communities, Tactical Tech asks human rights advocates what they are doing, what they want to do and then strategises with them to assess how ICT can help to increase the impact of their work; members of the collective then design, re-mix, translate, localise and re-appropriate content, training, tools and tactics to meet specific needs and contexts.

Tactical Tech had been including mobiles in various training activities since early 2003. Through this work it had become apparent that many human rights advocates believed that mobile phones offered new possibilities for communicating, organising and disseminating information to some of the world's poorest people. But it was also clear that obstacles presented by the existing technological and commercial landscape – including a lack of cheap, easy-to-use and applicable software and services – limited the ability of campaigners to fully exploit these opportunities in their work. Because of this, Tactical Tech began investigating possible partnerships that would support mobile advocacy in the global South. In 2006 Tactical Tech and Fahamu made a decision to collaborate, and soon after they were awarded funding from Hivos and the Open Society Institute for a project to establish an African network of mobile activists. Tactical Tech's role in this project was to develop a mobile phone toolkit for distribution in Africa. The toolkit needed to be designed for use both online and offline – in the form of a website and CD-ROM and booklet – to ensure that the content was accessible to those with and without internet connectivity. It was also decided that it must be published in both English and French to broaden its reach.

Mobiles in-a-box, designed to support campaigners to use mobile telephony in their work, became Tactical Tech's fourth toolkit. It followed Message in-a-box, a set of strategic guides and tools to create media for social change; the Security edition of NGO in-a-box, designed to meet the digital security and privacy needs of human rights defenders and independent media; and NGO in-a-box, a collection of tools for the day-to-day running of small- to medium-sized NGOs. Tactical Tech has also produced a number of other guides including *Maps for Advocacy*, *Visualising Information for Advocacy* and the *Quick 'n' Easy Guide to Online Advocacy*. Together these toolkits and guides have been translated from English into six other languages including French, Spanish, Portuguese, Farsi, Arabic and Russian.

Participatory development in action

The participation of grassroots human rights advocates is critical to Tactical Tech's approach to developing tools, guides, services and training. Participatory development involves the end users of a product or service in the design process to help ensure that what is done and created meets their needs and is founded upon their collective knowledge and experiences. Tactical Tech co-founder, Marek Tuszynski, describes Tactical Tech's style of participatory development as being 'very inclusive':

> For Tactical Tech our participatory development process begins by asking human rights advocates what they are doing and what they want to do better. We then develop ways to bring together technologists and advocates so that they can look at what tactics and technology are available and suitable to address their needs. End users of our toolkits and services are supported to participate in all stages of the development process and they are always appropriately credited for their involvement.[2]

The participatory development process used to create toolkits at Tactical Tech has evolved over a number of years. As Figure 4.1 illustrates, there are four key stages involved: research and listen; consult and collaborate; create and distribute; and evaluate and reflect. This illustration uses simple metaphors to highlight the participatory development process that was used to progress the development of the Mobiles in-a-box toolkit.

The following sections describe what happened during each stage of producing the Mobiles in-a-box toolkit, followed by reflections that highlight the key lessons learnt from this two-year participatory development process.

Research and listen

The first step taken to develop the Mobiles in-a-box toolkit involved assessing what was already happening in terms of mobile phone advocacy in Africa. Both Fahamu and Tactical Tech

Figure 4.1 Participatory development of toolkits and guides

began carrying out literature reviews and talking with human rights-focused organisations and advocates in late 2006.[3] This research process yielded useful insights into the complexity of the mobile landscape and the lack of accessible mobile telephony tools and affordable services that existed for human rights advocates.

In tandem with this research a call was widely distributed for applicants to attend a three-day start-up workshop on establishing an African network of mobile activists and a follow-up, two-day mobile advocacy toolkit working meeting in Nairobi. Responses to this call were received from around the world from developers working in mobile applications in the not-for-profit and commercial sector, as well as from NGOs, funders and activists. From these responses, a short list of invitees were supported to attend; collectively, they incorporated experience working in human rights and the NGO sector in Africa and in developing mobile applications.

The workshop, held in May 2007, brought together more than 40 technologists, activists, academics and civil society practitioners from all over the African continent to explore ways that mobile technology could contribute to advocacy work. Crucially, the participants were able to ensure that their own local and country contexts and needs were considered in the toolkit development process. For example, privacy, security and exposure emerged as important issues that would need to be addressed by the toolkit, given the threat of violence, conflict, intimidation and corruption that some human rights campaigners had to mediate in carrying out their advocacy work. Government policies were also found to provide stifling barriers that needed to be considered. In Ethiopia, for example, text messages were banned between 2005 and 2007 after they were used to mobilise during an election campaign, and Zimbabwean participants discussed legislation in their country that allowed the government to monitor activities across mobile networks. The workshop participants' collective knowledge provided countless insights into the economic, legal, political, social and technical issues that human rights advocates needed to consider if mobile telephony was to be appropriate and safe to use in their work. The value of the workshop as part of the overall design process is emphasised by these comments made by workshop participants Kevin Nnandi and Christiana Charles-Iyoha:

> Before the mobile advocacy workshop in Nairobi, I had been doing some work with mobile phones without realising the potential in telephony at my disposal in development work. The Nairobi meeting provided that tonic in promoting the use of mobile phones for increased communication, networking amongst organisations and coping with capacity gaps...One big lesson from the workshop is that there is no end to the use of mobile tactics.[4]
> The Nairobi meeting [was] critical because it was a meeting of both techies and non-techies like me who actually interact with people whose literacy levels as well as understanding of complex technology equipment are, at best, limited. The meeting therefore afforded me the opportunity [to understand] how the technology works beyond voice, SMS, MMS and the data bit I was used to and to consider how an NGO or community groups can take advantage of this technology.[5]

At the end of this workshop an email-supported network, PAMONET, was established by Fahamu and Tactical Tech with a number of interested organisations. The idea was that this network would support information and knowledge sharing among technologists and advocates and that this, in turn, would foster broader collaboration among the workshop participants in the mobile toolkit's ongoing development. It is important to acknowledge here that PAMONET has not been very active since it was established. The reasons for this require a longer discussion that is beyond the scope of this chapter. However, it is likely that PAMONET needed more resource investment to ensure that it was active and relevant to the workshop participants' needs and interests, and more consideration was needed to assess the factors that would be required to grow and sustain a dynamic and successful online community of interest.

Consult and collaborate

At the mobile advocacy toolkit working meeting 25 participants who had attended the workshop were invited to spend an additional two days in Nairobi developing an appropriate structure and identifying content needs for the toolkit. Participatory sessions provided an opportunity for human rights advocates to explain what they needed and expected from a mobile toolkit. These sessions established that the participants wanted guides that were structured not around particular technologies but around scenarios – such as the need to gather or disseminate information about specific issues. The sessions also highlighted that some people attending the meeting were keenly interested in, but largely unaware of, many of the potential applications of mobile technology in their work. This in turn emphasised the need for materials to be pitched at non-technologists. A content team was established which included ten technologists and advocacy practitioners based in eight different countries including Kenya, South Africa and Uganda. This team brought together expertise in human rights advocacy and the NGO sector in Africa, practical experience in developing mobile applications for the NGO and activist sector, and proficient skills in communicating complex technical issues.

Those who attended the meeting felt that they were able not only to contribute to the development of a toolkit that would practically support their work, but also to share insights, strategies and tools with one another. Ken Banks, creator of FrontlineSMS[6] (see Chapter 3 of this book), a free bulk mobile messaging tool designed for NGOs, attended the workshop and meeting and later became a member of the content team. He explains the value of this meeting in the toolkit development process:

> The initial meeting was an essential step in determining what the toolkit needed to look like and do, and what it did not. With so many tools which may or may not qualify as 'mobile' it was a great opportunity to determine priorities, criteria for inclusion and categories, and get the perspectives of a wide number of people from diverse backgrounds.[7]

Christiana Charles-Iyoha, from the Centre for Policy and Development[8] in Nigeria, also felt that the workshop and meeting were crucial to her later involvement as a member of the toolkit's content team:

> Everyone was given an opportunity to share ideas and experiences which were all analysed. Most importantly, the process … really helped those of us non-techies to grasp the fundamentals of the technology to see how it can be better applied to our work.[9]

Create

After the Nairobi workshop and meeting, the editorial team spent the next seven months working to prepare the content for the toolkit using email, VOIP and a project wiki. This involved selecting the technology tools to be included in the toolkit and sending them to be tested on multiple platforms and categorised for their appropriateness and functionality.

Working across countries and time zones, without the opportunity for face-to-face meetings, the content team wrote all the text for the toolkit based on the structure and needs that had been established at the Nairobi workshop and meeting. This way of working presented challenges but these were considered less important than ensuring the right expert mix of technologists and advocates.

The use of a wiki to share and develop the tools and content was critical to the participatory process employed by Tactical Tech. The wiki format allowed all members of the content team to create and edit content in an open and transparent fashion – since all edits and modifications to wiki content are rendered visible. The wiki was also used to allow an editorial team and other interested parties to read and comment on the content as it was written.

Additionally, a group of technologists from the Philippines, led by Roberto Soriano, was responsible for testing all the tools selected by the content team on a diverse range of mobile and computer platforms. They then categorised these tools according to how many platforms they served as well as their usability level in terms of installation, configuration and use.

Meanwhile, as the content team was busy putting together a draft of the toolkit, Fahamu promoted opportunities for African human rights organisations to be involved in testing the toolkit. Four organisations were selected on the basis of their commitment to and interest in exploring new possibilities for using mobile phones in their advocacy work. The four organisations also worked in different geographic and thematic areas in Africa and had different ICT needs, resources and skills. This diversity would test the flexibility and usability of the Mobiles toolkit.

The organisations were: the Made in Kenya Network, based in Nairobi;[10] the International Centre for Accelerated Development (ICAD), based in Kebbi State, Nigeria; the Women of Uganda Network[11] (WOUGNET) (for more on WOUGNET, see Chapter 8), based in Kampala; and the Congolese Law Clinic for Justice and Reconciliation (CLCJR), based in Lubumbashi, Democratic Republic of Congo. Each organisation was employed for six weeks to evaluate the toolkit. During the time they tested the technology tools and assessed the relevance of the strategies and other content to their work, they were provided with access to the content team to talk through problems and concerns. At the end of the testing period the organisations completed a report that provided detailed and specific feedback on all aspects of the draft toolkit. The detail included in the feedback is highlighted in this quote from Made in Kenya:

The software challenge [using FrontlineSMS] was in getting the drivers for a Nokia 6070, while the hardware challenge was in getting the appropriate CA-42 cable ... We needed support in installing the correct version ... It is worthwhile to note that the use of BulkSMS.com requires credit cards that are usually limited in circulation in developing countries.[12]

Each of the organisations also imparted nuanced understandings regarding the way the same technological application was being used in different ways to address local needs and realities. For example, WOUGNET wrote:

A missed call (beeping) is practically an accepted form of communication in Uganda, especially when a pre-arranged activity/event happens. For example, I'll beep you when I'm free and we can meet at place X. It's also used to indicate that I'd like to speak to you, but I haven't got enough credit/airtime for the conversation, can you call me back?[13]

A slightly different use of the mobile phone to get someone to call you without incurring a charge was noted by CLCJR:

Another use of mobile is the 'please recharge me' [message] option provide[d] by Vodacom. This free option is used as a 'call me back'. Every Vodacom subscriber has five 'please recharge me' per day.[14]

One of the toolkit features most appreciated by the four testing organisations was the use of case studies that highlighted real examples where mobile telephony had been used for advocacy. Each organisation was able to suggest new case study examples including their own organisation's experiences; they were all also able to tell a story of how the toolkit had enhanced their advocacy work during the testing period. For example, ICAD had been using mobiles for some time to send messages that provided information about HIV/AIDS and reproductive health to people who were HIV positive. Before using the toolkit ICAD would send out messages individually to people. After their use of the toolkit, they began using FrontlineSMS to send out bulk alerts that informed people of health services that would be coming to their area, and bulk messages to provide people with information on HIV, including the prevention of mother to-child-transmission and methods for care and support. CLCJR also began using FrontlineSMS as part of its toolkit testing process and they made plans to establish a network of young people who could use the bulk service to address bullying in schools. WOUGNET reported that it used FrontlineSMS to support an SMS discussion among 100 individuals drawn from government, the private sector and civil society on the use of ICT in poverty reduction, while they also made plans to draw from the toolkit to carry out fundraising activities. The Made in Kenya network stated that, as a result of its involvement, it had applied ShoZu (www.shozu.com) to document and publicise its work on CNN and Facebook, and had used fring (www.fring.com) to enable low-cost mobile phone Skype communication among staff. It also launched BungeSMS,[15] a website allowing Kenyan voters to send SMS messages to report on corruption.

Through these practical applications of the toolkit each organisation was able to share insights and technical experiences and to make suggestions for modifications. As a result, considerable changes were subsequently made to the toolkit including the addition of new content and case studies and the removal of tools that required skills that were considered to be beyond the scope of the intended audience.

The final toolkit is now available online in both French and English (see http://mobiles.tacticaltech.org/) and 1,000 hard copies have been printed for distribution to human rights campaigners in the global South. Distribution hubs run by African NGOs in Nigeria, Uganda and Kenya have been established to distribute hard copies of the toolkit to partner organisations and beneficiaries of their work. The toolkit is also being widely promoted to advocacy, activist and alternative media organisations and networks. While the focus for distribution is on the global South, many North-based NGOs have also reported that they are using the online version. The toolkit uses a creative commons licence[16] that supports not-for-profit organisations and activists to appropriate and re-mix the content for their own purposes; a number of NGOs have reported that they have done this.

Evaluate and reflect

While four organisations have reported on the Mobiles in-a-box toolkit as part of the testing process, it is also important to Tactical Tech that stories and experiences based on the toolkit's practical application are collected over time so that they can be shared with other advocates and integrated into future updated versions of the toolkit.

Short evaluation questionnaires are distributed with every hard copy of the toolkit and are available for those who use the online version. User questionnaire feedback is to be regularly analysed by Tactical Tech, not only to consider the impacts of the toolkit and how it can be updated and improved in future editions but also to assess what kinds of additional support NGOs and advocates require to effectively use mobile phone technology for social change. However, getting people to voluntarily complete and return these evaluations is proving difficult and unfortunately this makes measuring the mobile toolkit's outreach and impact a real challenge. For this reason, while Tactical Tech will persist with seeking new and engaging ways that support people to provide user feedback in a way that is convenient to them (using, for example, postcards, online forms, chat and Skype calls), there is now also a shifting focus to quality rather than quantity in terms of the monitoring and evaluation methods used. Tactical Tech therefore, beyond analysing the short evaluation questionnaires, has allocated project funds so that at least six human rights organisations or advocates will be paid to creatively document how they apply the Mobiles in-a-box toolkit to their advocacy work. They will do this using video, audio, animation, photographs, visual diagrams or text. These advocates will also complete a much more extensive evaluation questionnaire that documents the specific technology they used as well as the technical, social, political or financial issues they encountered. Over time these creative stories of mobile advocacy made by NGOs and human rights campaigners will be linked to the online version of the Mobiles in-a-box toolkit to inspire and support new campaigns in other places.

The future of mobile advocacy in Africa

The participatory development process used by Tactical Tech to create a toolkit that responds to the needs of human rights advocates in Africa provides some insights into the way an inclusive, bottom–up approach can be used to address the needs of frontline NGOs and human rights advocates working in marginalised communities. The participatory process highlighted that abundant opportunities and enthusiasm exist for using mobile telephony to support human rights work in Africa. Mobiles in-a-box now provides the information, tools and tactics that are required to realise many of these opportunities. There remain, of course, other factors that continue to work against these opportunities including poor telecommunications infrastructure, high cost burdens, a lack of affordable mobile telephony training and support services, and increasing levels of state surveillance in some countries that inhibit some NGOs and activists involved in sensitive human rights work. Further work also needs to be done to build and strengthen mobile advocacy networks in Africa in order to support information and knowledge sharing as well as greater collaboration and support services. As evidence of barriers and needs emerges through the Mobiles in-a-box monitoring and evaluation process, Tactical Tech will work with others to find new, participatory and creative ways to address them by bringing together human rights advocates and technologists and asking them: What are you doing? What can we do better?

Notes

1. An e-rider is a 'roving NGO ICT consultant' who provides specialist support across a number of like-minded NGOs and also supports information, knowledge-sharing and collaboration among them. (see: http://www.eriders.net).
2. Tuszynski, Marek (2009) email interview, 27 January.
3. Fahamu's literature review and pre-workshop planning document can be found at: http://mobileactive.org/wiki/images/f/fb/African_Mobile_Activism.pdf, accessed 1 February 2009.
4. Nnandi, Kevin (2009) email interview, 26 January.
5. Charles-Iyoha, Christiana (2009) email interview, 23 January.
6. http://www.frontlinesms.com/.
7. Banks, Ken (2009) email interview, 23 January.
8. http://poldec.org/.

9. Charles-Iyoha, Christiana (2009) email interview, 24 January.
10. http://www.madeinkenya.org/.
11. http://www.wougnet.org/.
12. Made in Kenya (2008) *Testing Evaluation Report.*
13. WOUGNET (2008) *Testing Evaluation Report.*
14. CLCJR (2008) *Testing Evaluation Report.*
15. http://www.bungesms.com/about.html.
16. http://creativecommons.org/.

Acknowledgments

The authors would like to thank Media Shala (http://www.mediashala.com/)
from Ahmedabad for helping Tactical Tech to create the illustration provided
in this chapter. We would like to acknowledge that much of this chapter
was drafted from notes posted on the project wiki by all those involved in
creating the toolkit. Additional and valuable inputs were provided by Ken
Banks, Kevin Nnandi, Christiana Charles-Iyoha and Toni Eliasz. We would
also like to thank everyone who contributed to the Mobiles in-a-box project
and acknowledge that this was made possible with the support of Fahamu
and funding assistance from Hivos and Open Society Institute.

5

Fahamu: using cell phones in an activist campaign

Redante Asuncion-Reed

Introduction

It is a common assertion that social media technology has utterly transformed communications. This technology has allowed people and organisations to communicate, organise and mobilise quickly in ways that were not previously feasible. This chapter describes, analyses and assesses one organisation's experience with using a particular type of social media-mobile phone text messaging in social activism. The question I seek to answer is: Can the use of social media make activist groups more effective in reaching their objectives?

Very little academic research has been done on the application of social media in political and social activism. Most of the published materials come not from scholars but from practitioners in the field who are actively using and experimenting with this technology and sharing best practices. Very few of these works also focus on the increasingly popular use of mobile phones in activism in the global South areas of the world, where the penetration of mobile phones significantly dwarfs the use of internet technology. This chapter, therefore, seeks to lay the groundwork for future research.

Background

In recent years, the deployment of mobile phones as tools in political mobilisation and activism in some countries has gained attention from the mainstream media. The most celebrated cases of activist success via cell phone mobilisation were the toppling of the administration of President Joseph Estrada in the Philippines (also known as the People Power II revolution); the election and restoration to the presidency following impeachment of Roh Moo-hyun in South Korea, where text messaging and the internet-driven alternative media were instrumental; and in Kuwait, where text messaging and Blackberries were used by women to mobilise in record numbers to win the right to vote.[1]

Such dramatic success stories give rise to interest in the effectiveness of this new tool. Have mobile phones been used in other places and in other ways, and with what effect? How does one measure and determine success – are quantifiable metrics and measures of audience engagement sufficient or appropriate? How can its contribution to social change be determined and tracked?

Mainstream media reports on mobile phone activism focus on the drama: the techniques and methods that produce spectacular and compelling results. Journalist Mary Jordan, for example, sees cell phones and text messaging changing the ways that political mobilisation is done around the world:

> From Manila to Riyadh and Kathmandu, protests once publicised on coffeehouse bulletin boards are now organised entirely through text-messaging networks that can reach vast numbers of people in a matter of minutes.[2]

These few examples make a compelling case for studying social media – particularly mobile phones – in social and political activism. While much attention has been paid to the phenomenon of social media in activism, very little actual research has been done to establish a baseline of knowledge about the effectiveness of such tools in action.

Fahamu

Fahamu is an African NGO established in 1997 by Kenyan social activist and current executive director, Firoze Manji. It has offices in Oxford in the UK, Kenya, South Africa and Senegal. Fahamu is a Kiswahili word that means 'understanding'. The organisation is a pioneer in using emerging technology in support of human rights and social justice.[3]

Fahamu's work covers four broad areas:

- Innovative use of information and communication technology
- Stimulating debate, discussion and analysis
- Distributing news and information
- Developing training materials and running distance-learning courses.

Fahamu focuses primarily on Africa, although it collaborates with other organisations such as Oxfam, the Office of the United Nations High Commissioner for Human Rights, and the Ford Foundation, to support the global movement for human rights and social justice.[4]

Fahamu has received a number of awards for its use of technology in activism. Fahamu was one of five Tech Laureates in the 2005 Microsoft Education Award category. Its online newsletter, Pambazuka News, won the Highway Africa 2005 award for the innovative use of new media. The organisation also won the AOL Innovations in the Community Award 2004 for innovations in the use of SMS for advocacy work. Fahamu South Africa was one of ten winners of the Gender and Agriculture in the Information Society (GenARDIS) 2005 Award. Fahamu was runner-up for the Stockholm Challenge 2004 award for the development of distance learning courses for human rights organisations. And finally, in the PoliticsOnline and sixth Worldwide Forum on Electronic Democracy, Pambazuka News was in 2005 recognised as one of the top ten individuals, organisations and companies who are changing the world of the internet and politics.[5]

Fahamu and mobile phones

Recognised as being at the forefront of e-advocacy not only in Africa but globally,[6] Fahamu's cell phone campaigns have attracted wide attention in technology circles and among activists who advocate using emerging technology in social justice work.

In 2004, Fahamu joined Solidarity with African Women's Rights (SOAWR), an NGO coalition composed of 21 women's and human rights organisations, to promote the ratification of the Protocol on the Rights of Women in Africa. The protocol is international legislation that guarantees African women's rights.

Fahamu offered technological support and the use of Pambazuka News to the coalition to raise public awareness about the protocol. It created a website and developed procedures for people to register their support for the protocol using mobile text messaging (SMS) technology. An SMS alert service was also established which enabled users to sign up for free SMS alerts about the progress of the campaign. The goal of ratification by 15 countries in the African Union was achieved, enabling the protocol to be ratified on November 2005.[7]

The protocol campaign

The Protocol on the Rights of Women in Africa was the group's very first SMS campaign and, as far as the organisers knew, was the first time SMS technology had been used in such a fashion.[8]

Fahamu set up a phone number in South Africa to receive text messages. Those signing the petition text messaged the word 'petition' along with the caller's name and telephone number to the designated phone number in South Africa. The sim card, attached to a computer, converted the message to an email and placed it in a send box. A script was written to check the send box frequently. The contents were then delivered to a database and stored. Once in the database, the information could be presented in any method Fahamu chose. A list of the signatories was displayed online on the Fahamu website throughout the campaign and was also presented to the African Union.[9]

The campaign was first publicised in the Pambazuka News newsletter. International ties with feminist and human rights organisations were utilised as the campaign was promoted internationally in conferences and meetings with like-minded social justice organisations. The final push was provided by international mainstream media as articles published in the BBC spiked the number of petitions upward in the latter end of the campaign.

The campaign collected 4,000 signatures – fewer than 450 of them from SMS text messages – from 29 African countries. Despite the relatively low number of petitioners, the campaign was widely considered a success. Before the campaign, only one country had ratified the protocol. Within one year of the campaign being launched, the goal of the required 15 countries ratifying the protocol was reached.[10]

Fahamu's executive director, Firoze Manji, likened their initial foray into mobile phone activism to a blind person tapping around with a white stick.

> We didn't have a clue what would happen, or what the reception would be ... It was just such a crazy idea and, even if it didn't work, out of failures, you learn. Some of the best stuff we've done has come out of stuff that's gone badly ... We thought we'd done something run-of-the-mill, that everyone here at MobileActive would have done something like this long ago ... But it turned out it's something no-one else has ever done. This is new technology, it's growing all the time – so the potential is growing all the time.[11]

Global Call to Action against Poverty campaign

Fahamu launched a second SMS campaign in 2005 in support of the Global Call to Action against Poverty (GCAPSMS) (www.whiteband.org/), an international confederation of organisations calling for cancellation of African debt to the developed nations of the global North. The GCAPSMS campaign was the African component of the international Make Poverty History campaign, which was started in 2005 in the UK. The Make Poverty History campaign was an international coalition of charities, religious groups, trade unions, campaigning groups and celebrities who mobilised to increase awareness and to pressure governments into taking action towards eradicating poverty. The symbol of the campaign was a white bracelet. Television ads in Europe, the United States, and in other countries ran for many months, urging people to speak to their representatives about the issue of the poverty and debt of countries in the global South to institutions such as the International Monetary Fund and the World Bank.[12]

For this campaign, Fahamu enhanced the SMS technology to be able to send longer text messages and for every SMS message to be displayed in a section of the GCAPSMS website. Concerts and musical events, featuring Africa's most prominent musicians, and held to coincide with important meetings of world bodies such as the United Nations and the World Trade Organisation, were broadcast on television throughout Africa. During the concerts, viewers were called upon to text 'No to Debt', along with a plea to end poverty in their own words, to a number that then displayed the messages on the GCAPSMS website.[13]

The website highlighted Fahamu's technological strengths: it included content from Pambazuka News, regularly updated SMS messages from all over the world, as well as an RSS feed of these messages.[14] More than 2,000 SMS messages were received on the GCAPSMS website after the project launched in 2005.[15]

Analysis

Mobile phones for SMS campaigns were a strategic choice for Fahamu. There were approximately 52 million mobile phone subscribers in Africa as of January 2004 with a projected 67 million by the end of 2005. The campaigns provided the opportunity to test whether this population of texters could be mobilised for a social justice campaign.[16] The report, 'Prospects for e-Advocacy in the Global South', supports these figures that indicate a skyrocketing growth of mobile phone penetration in Africa. It argues that while poorer nations continue to have lower penetration rates than richer ones, poorer nations also exhibit vastly higher growth rates. For example, while the UK's mobile phone use grew by 23 per cent between 2002 and 2004, Nigeria's grew by 537 per cent.[17]

According to Fahamu's executive director, Manji:

> We decided to use SMS as a way of enabling people to sign an online petition. This technology has not previously been used before (to our knowledge, and certainly not in Africa) … We had no expectations that we would have got thousands or even millions of SMS messages (and that would have bankrupted us if we had!). No the point was that we wanted to get public attention as part of our overall campaign to get the protocol ratified by the necessary 15 countries so that it would come into force.[18]

More than just a petition or a tool to collect signatures, Fahamu realised the value of enacting the campaign for the Protocol on the Rights of Women in Africa was a way to gain publicity for the cause.

For the GCAPSMS campaign, Fahamu amplified this strategic use of technology by augmenting the SMS technology to allow for longer text messages, and publishing the text messages they received on a website, www.gcapsms.org/,[19] created for that purpose. Publicising and cross-marketing the website and the SMS text message number in conjunction with large-scale music festivals and concerts [20] resulted in widespread media attention and international recognition for their innovative use of technology and, by extension, for the cause for which they were using the technology.

The resources that Fahamu used to implement the campaigns were a part-time programmer and part time information officer over an 18-month period. Their basic equipment was a cell phone sim card attached to a computer. In terms of special skills or technology, code was written to transfer information from the sim card to a database. All of this was implemented at a cost of approximately US$10,000. This outline gives an idea of the scope of Fahamu as an organisation, that is, one of modest resources and size.

Although Fahamu's goal for these campaigns was to mobilise the African population to sign their petition (this had never been done before, inside or outside Africa, and certainly not on the scale that Fahamu attempted), their main focus was to channel the publicity that they received as a result of the campaigns to amplify and to gain attention for their cause. Was Fahamu successful? If so, how was success defined? How was it measured?

Campaign results vs objectives

The numerical results of Fahamu's petition campaigns were that 4,000 signed the petition for the protocol of which about 500 came from text messages. About 2,000 signatures were gathered for the GCAPSMS campaign. In the case of the protocol campaign, within one year of starting the campaign, the required 15 nations ratified the legislation for the protocol to come into force. This was the main intention and the primary measure of success for the campaign. For the GCAPSMS campaign, the publicity that Fahamu received as a result of the campaign widely publicised the Make Poverty History movement. Moreover, they were able to gain considerable attention in the media and among technology and activist circles.

Examples of the international attention they received came from MobileActive, where the two campaigns were featured in the Strategy Guide for Using Mobile Phones in Advocacy Campaigns,[21] DemoBlog,[22] BBC News,[23] WorldChanging,[24] Personal Democracy Forum,[25] and Tactical Technology Collective,[26] among others. According to Firoze Manji, this international attention for the causes, more than the act of collecting signatures, was the main objective for conducting both campaigns.

If one were to judge Fahamu's SMS campaigns solely on numerical metrics, their results were very modest. They accumulated fewer than 5,000 signatures for each petition campaign from a population base of tens of millions of potential petition signers. It can be argued that Fahamu could have attained better numerical results had its campaign been conducted differently. They could have used better messaging to appeal to a wider base of people. They could have taken advantage of better ways to deliver their message to let more people know about the campaign. The campaigns, with bigger budgets, could have been marketed to a larger segment of the African population. The delivery methods used and target audiences for the campaign may have been too narrow.

Fahamu's executive director, Firoze Manji, provides some insight into Fahamu's thinking in assessing the results of the campaigns:

> The tool that we used was SMS/petition. But the 'metric' we used to measure the success of our campaign was, from the start, to have the necessary 15 countries ratify the protocol and for the protocol to come into force. That was the outcome we were looking for. We were looking to build up a movement. The absolute number of SMS messages we received was relatively small (some 500 only, although quite a number of those represented messages from organisations with hundreds, and in some cases, thousands, of members). But the publicity we got, especially when famous people like Graça Machel signed, was considerable. We had lots of interviews in the mainstream press, and each such interview provided us with an opportunity to promote the cause (not the technology!).[27]

This is a good place to make a distinction between measuring the effectiveness of a particular cell phone campaign and measuring the results from using cell phones as a tool for social change. One can set up an SMS campaign to gather important data. One can track the number of opt-in rates, the number of people who responded to the campaign's SMS message, the number of times the SMS was forwarded, the number of downloads of ring tones from the campaign website, among other indicators. These can all be considered important metrics that are measurable indicators of how successful a campaign was in attracting and mobilising people to some sort of action.

Fahamu monitored the petition signatures. The number of petitions gathered, although small in quantitative terms, had big consequences. For the protocol campaign, the 4,000 signatures that Fahamu gathered, coupled with the public relations push that gave high visibility to the effort, proved sufficient in spurring the required 15 nations to ratify the protocol legislation. The protocol campaign, therefore, was successful in attaining its stated goal as well as giving Fahamu the experience of launching such a campaign.

It is less clear whether the GCAPSMS campaign succeeded in its stated goal to address poverty. One would have to see these efforts as tied to the larger Make Poverty History movement. But if one were to keep in mind that the stated goal of Fahamu was not collecting as many signatures as possible but to attract attention to an important cause, then one can contend that the attention the GCAPSMS campaign received was its own measure of success.

One could make the argument, however, that the nature of Fahamu's activism was not utterly changed by the introduction of social media technology of cell phones and SMS. Theirs was not a technological revolution in activist methods because they still relied on the traditional activist tactic of gaining publicity for their cause as their primary objective in undertaking the campaigns.

The point, for Fahamu, is that there are now new methods, strategies, and tools that an organisation can choose to deploy to advance its cause. An SMS campaign using cell phones is one such method. It can be combined with traditional activist methods, such as publicity, as Fahamu did. The question at the end is the same: Did the organisation accomplish what it set out to do? Fahamu did succeed in accomplishing what it set out to do.

Another criticism one can make is that Fahamu's SMS campaigns were not particularly effective ways of mobilising, organising or communicating and, hence, not an innovation in the way technology was used. Judging from the modest quantitative results of gathering signatures, the population of African texters were not mobilised in great numbers to join the cause.

But it is clear that Fahamu's SMS campaigns were experimental. Fahamu's use of technology was innovative for its time. No other organisation had ever attempted to do what they set out to do with the methods they used. The fact that Fahamu initiated these campaigns and received worldwide attention for their effort builds a foundation for future campaigns using SMS and cell phone technology.

What is notable about Fahamu's efforts is the impact generated from a modest investment of US$10,000, basic communications equipment and a staff of two part-time workers. Fahamu's campaigns provide lessons in networking, public relations and marketing as much as the innovative use of technology. In addition, Fahamu demonstrated how the creative and strategic use of technology can allow a small organisation with limited means to accomplish great things. Its role in the ratification of international law for women's rights through the protocol campaign is a significant feat for any organisation. Fahamu's modest resources were skilfully invested in accomplishing a strategic objective while testing new possibilities of a technological tool.

SMS campaigns after Fahamu

Technology and techniques for cell phone SMS campaigns have evolved by leaps and bounds since Fahamu's initial, experimental forays into the medium in 2004. SMS campaigns have been growing in sophistication following in the footsteps of commercial SMS marketing campaigns. Large NGOs with substantial budgets such as Amnesty International, Oxfam, International Fund for Animal Welfare (IFAW) and Greenpeace have undertaken SMS campaigns since Fahamu.

IFAW's 2006 campaign to create a popular groundswell against the Canadian practice of seal-hunting garnered 50,000 mobile petition signatures. Oxfam mobilised over 100,000 protesters in June 2005 for the G8 Summit in Edinburgh, Scotland, in a campaign that made extensive use of mobile phone messaging.[28] Amnesty International USA combined traditional advertising with an SMS campaign in a 2007 petition campaign urging Congress to close the US Guantanamo Bay detention centre. They published a full-page advertisement in the *New York Times* which urged readers to text in their support.[29] The 2005 Zero Waste campaign by Greenpeace Argentina asked people to send an SMS to support the formation of a group of 'mobile-activistas' to promote their campaign. These mobile activists sent text messages to legislatures and key players involved in the various hearings. SMS was also used to arrange spontaneous meeting points and demonstrations. The result: the government of Buenos Aires will implement a Zero Waste policy that will reduce urban waste sent to landfills by 50 per cent by 2010, 75 per cent by 2015 and 100 per cent by 2020.[30] While Fahamu can be considered a pioneer in SMS campaigning, these large organisations can now be considered the leaders.

The dynamics of SMS campaigning have also changed since Fahamu did the groundwork. SMS campaigns such as those cited in the previous paragraph have been conducted with bigger budgets. They have become more sophisticated in targeting and segmenting audiences, crafting messages to appeal to different audience segments, delivering messages, collecting data to measure different indicators of audience engagement, establishing metrics to determine the effectiveness of campaigns, and creating cross-promotion strategies for keeping people engaged in campaigns. Finally, technology to implement SMS campaigns are increasingly outsourced to companies that specialise in such campaigns:[31] companies now exist which handle the implementation, evaluation and technical aspects of SMS campaigning and which cater to the NGO market.

More recent SMS campaigns by NGOs have been able to demonstrate quantifiable results in the tens of thousands in terms of petition signatures, opt-ins to their networks, and downloads of ringtones and wallpapers, among others. The techniques of commercial campaigns have filtered into the NGO sector and, many would argue, to great effect. With increasing sophistication, however, come greater expectations of new techniques and technology to effect social change, the fundamental reason that activists conduct SMS campaigns in the first place.

Evaluating whether current SMS campaigns are fulfilling the promise of social media as tools for organising, mobilising, and communicating is still a big challenge for activists. Measuring these developments would have to begin by inquiring whether the campaigns are engaging their audiences in meaningful ways and whether this correlates to taking action, again, in meaningful ways and in sufficient numbers.

These challenges point to directions for future research on the implications for other organisations that choose to use this technology of what has been learned from Fahamu's innovations in using social media. A survey of organisations that use social media technology would be a good start. Some research questions could be: Are these organisations accomplishing their goals? Are they able to enact campaigns that were impossible or unrealistic before the introduction of social media technology? Are they able to reach people or exchange information in ways not thought possible without these tools?

A similar survey can also be conducted among organisations that do not use social media technology. Future research will always go back to the basic questions for any social movement or social change organisation: How does one know if one's efforts have been successful?

The best way to measure success – and by extension, the effectiveness of social media tools – is to check accomplishments against stated goals. This simple rule of thumb should compel disciplined, strategic thinking and imaginative use of limited resources. Whether it is to ratify a piece of legislation or to call attention to poverty, one must always keep the end results in mind in evaluating the effectiveness of technology.

There also must be caution against focusing too much on the use of technology as a magic formula. According to Firoze Manji of Fahamu, 'It is easy to be romantic about the tools, their potential, and capabilities. The point is to be strategic, and recognise that tools only complement, and do not substitute for, human interaction.'[32]

Conclusion

This study is an attempt to lay the foundations for future research and exploration in the role of social media technology in activism for social change. Directions for future research, therefore, should look at applications of social media technology by other activist organisations. Do organisations that use social media also see a measure of success far beyond their capabilities in the absence of these tools? Do organisations that use social media use them effectively and in ways that allow them to accomplish their goals? Is access to social media allowing them to set goals for themselves that would be unrealistic in the absence of these tools, given their scope and budgets? And how does the track record of organisations that use social media compare with the track record of those that do not use these tools? Are social media-using organisations doing a better job overall? Only further research and empirical comparisons would yield answers to these questions.

Fahamu illustrated how the adoption and use of social media tools can allow an organisation to accomplish much more than is usually possible given the scope and budget of most non-profit and activist organisations. The technology had a levelling effect where a small organisation like Fahamu can have the potential to accomplish big things. If Fahamu can accomplish what it has with the technology, it is that much more exciting to speculate about, and to explore, how much social media activism can accomplish when utilised by larger organisations with bigger budgets such as Greenpeace and Amnesty International. Will the adage be true that bigger bucks will make for a bigger effect in the world of activism and social justice work? Or will the bigger effects be more a function of technical and strategic creativity, ingenuity, and resourcefulness? These questions offer exciting directions for further research.

Notes

1. Hong, C. (2005) 'New political tool: text messaging', *Christian Science Monitor*, 30 June, http://www.csmonitor.com/2005/0630/p13s01-stct.htm, accessed 20 March 2007.
2. Jordan, M. (2006)'Going mobile: text messages guide Filipino protesters', *Washington Post*, 25 August, http://www.washingtonpost.com/wp-dyn/content/article/2006/08/24/AR2006082401379_pf.html, accessed 13 September 2009.

3. Fahamu website, http://www.fahamu.org/aboutus.php, accessed 30 March 2007.

4. Ibid.

5. Fahamu (2005) *Annual Report 2004/2005*, p. 2.

6. DemoBlog (2006) 'Gates Project 12: Fahamu at the forefront', 26 October, http://internationaldemoblog.blogspot.com/2006/10/gates-project-12-fahamu-at-forefront.html, accessed 20 March 2007.

7. Fahamu (2005) *Annual Report 2004/2005*, p. 7.

8. Oberman, J. (2005) 'SMS, social justice style, in Africa', *Personal Democracy Forum*, 10 October, http://www.personaldemocracy.com/node/738, accessed 20 March 2007.

9. Ibid.

10. Fahamu, *Annual Report 2004/2005*, p. 9.

11. Gertz, E. 'Fahamu: Pan-African text messaging for social justice', *World Changing*, (31 October 2005), http://www.worldchanging.com/archives/003694.html, accessed 13 September 2009.

12. Wikipedia, 'Make Poverty History', http://en.wikipedia.org/wiki/Whiteband, accessed 4 April 2007.

13. Gertz, E. (2005).

14. Pambazuka News (2005) 'Africa: 40 million set to watch GCAP standing tall against poverty concert across Africa', 13 October, http://www.pambazuka.org/en/category/gcap/29828, accessed 11 April 2007.

15. GCAPSMS, 'Thumbs Down 2 Poverty', http://www.gcapsms.org/, accessed 30 March 2007.

16. Gertz, E. (2005).

17. Joyce, M. and Patel, R. (2007) 'Prospects for e-advocacy in the global South: a report for the Gates Foundation', *Version 1.0, Res Publica*, p. 18.

18. Firoze Manji (2007) e-mail message to author, 14 April.

19. Gertz, E. (2005).

20. Pambazuka News (2005) 13 October.

21. Stein, M. and Verclas, K. (2007) 'MobileActive.org strategy guide #2: Using mobile phones in advocacy campaigns, Strategy Guide Series', *MobileActive.org*, http://www.mobileactive.org/guides, accessed 25 March 2007.

22. DemoBlog (2006) 26 October.

23. BBC News (2004) 'Text petition for African women', 30 July, http://news.bbc.co.uk/2/hi/africa/3937715.stm, accessed 20 March 2007.

24. Gertz, E. (2005).

25. Oberman, J. (2005).

26. Noronha, F. (2006) 'From information to campaigning, an African network shows the way', Tactical Technology Collective, 2 November, http://www.tacticaltech.org/node/323, accessed 20 March 2007.

27. Firoze Manji, email to author.

28. Stein, M. and Verclas, K. (2007).

29. Textually.org (2007) 'Amnesty International launches SMS petition to close Guantanamo Bay', 12 January, http://www.textually.org/textually/

archives/2007/01/014667.htm, accessed 28 April 2007.

30. Mobileactive.org (2005) 'Congratulations Greenpeace Argentina!', 10 December, http://216.92.83.141/node/52, accessed 28 April 2007.

31. Examples of mobile campaign provider companies that service North American organisations are Mobile Accord (http://www.mobileaccord.com/) and Rights Group (http://www.rights-group.com/).

32. Firoze Manji, email to author.

6

The UmNyango project: using SMS for political participation in rural KwaZulu Natal

Anil Naidoo

Introduction

The majority of people living in KwaZulu Natal (KZN), South Africa's most populous province, live in rural areas, and most of them do not have access to adequate services. Out of the nine South African provinces, KZN is one of the three with the lowest human development index, highest unemployment rate and highest prevalence of HIV/AIDS.

Since the establishment of the democratic government in 1994, there have been numerous government strategies addressing the continuing problems of poverty and vulnerability, but their implementation has been problematic, mainly due to lack of adequate allocation of assets and resources. This has been further aggravated by the effects of apartheid and the HIV/AIDS pandemic.

The situation of women is particularly dire in KwaZulu Natal where, despite guarantees in the South African constitution, they still remain discriminated against by patriarchal systems that treat women as perpetual minors, even after they attain legal majority. This discrimination plays itself out in women's access to land and inheritance, and generally in their ability to be involved in development.

The emerging popular democratic movements in Africa need technology that will support their struggles, enabling them to network, build capacity and respect for human rights, share information, debate, discuss and collaborate. Mobile telephony

71

offers this potential and will result in the breaking down of barriers between communities and the enhancement of the capacity of groups to organise.

Currently, the use of mobile phones for voice communication is widespread in Africa and there are strong indications that mobile phone users are catching on to the global trend of using the SMS capability of their mobile phones to send text messages.

Fahamu (www.fahamu.org) has been experimenting with the potential of SMS technology to organise and mobilise members of social justice movements to better advocate for their rights. Fahamu showed in 2004 the potential of SMS technology as a tool for activism through its lead role in Solidarity for African Women's Rights, a coalition of 21 organisations that advocates for the ratification and implementation of the Protocol to the African Charter on Human and Peoples' Rights on the Rights of Women in Africa (see Chapter 5).

Given these successes, in 2005 Fahamu successfully proposed to the Gender and Agriculture in the Information Society (GenARDIS) awards committee, that it fund a pilot project to test the efficacy of SMS technology for rural-based women in KwaZulu Natal to access agricultural extension information for their sustainable livelihoods.

The purpose of the project was to test for the first time in rural KZN the potential of SMS technology as an information tool to empower rural women in agriculture to make more effective use of the limited resources available to them and to access development initiatives which they might not otherwise be aware of. The project concluded that indeed SMS technology could be effectively used by rural communities to access information.

In consequence, the UmNyango project was conceived by Fahamu as an integrated sustainable approach to promoting and protecting the rights of rural women in KZN. The project piloted access, for both women and men, to a human rights information and reporting system, using SMS technology. KZN was chosen as the geographic area of focus, due to its low development index in relation to other provinces, its history of political violence, the human rights situation of vulnerable groups, especially women and children in rural areas, as well as the presence of partners in KwaZulu Natal.

Our purpose was to test the feasibility of at least five rural communities in KZN being able to harness SMS technology in the local IsiZulu language, in order to:

- Enhance their potential for participation in regional, national, provincial and local government initiatives that impact on rural livelihoods and development. This was to include receiving, amongst other things, relevant headlines from Pambazuka News, Fahamu's award-winning electronic newsletter on social justice in Africa
- Contribute to overcoming the patriarchal challenges that make the reporting of violence against women virtually impossible
- Enable women's greater access to information on unconstitutional preclusion from land as well as land evictions, and to allow them to report on such unconstitutional conduct
- Enhance their participation in the early reporting of political tensions and violence
- Enhance their access to justice.

Implementing the project

Given the scope of human rights issues to be dealt with over a very large geographical area, the success of this project would be dependent on having access to requisite expertise as well as infrastructure. Our plan, therefore, included engaging five potential partners with expertise in the categories of human rights. The project was to target: participatory democracy, domestic violence, women's access and control of land, conflict resolution, and rural indigent access to justice. The following NGOs became our partners:

- Centre for Community Participation (CPP)
- Domestic Violence Assistance project (DVAP)
- Rural Women's Movement (RWM)
- Participative Development Initiative (PDI)
- Community Law and Rural Development Centre (CLRDC).

In the first phase we conducted a survey in the five communities to assess rural participants' attitudes towards using SMS and podcasting technology to promote and protect their human rights. From the GenARDIS project we were aware that rural women working in agriculture in KZN were willing to, and in fact did, make use of SMS technology for agricultural extension purposes. However, we were unsure whether this willingness could be extended to other rural areas and for a wider human rights focus.

The survey found that there is an 80 per cent IsiZulu literacy level, 83 per cent of respondents owned mobile phones and 80 per cent were able to send and retrieve basic text messages.

The network coverage was also healthy and reliable in the target communities. Of those surveyed, 84 per cent used the pre-paid method of accessing airtime. Seventy-six per cent used their mobile phones to make voice calls to follow up on social welfare, and water, sanitation and electricity applications, as well as to enquire about income-generating opportunities. The SMS facility was mostly used for personal purposes. Respondents did not use the SMS facility to access information on development initiatives nor on human rights. However, they welcomed any initiative that could allow them this opportunity, such as with the UmNyango project.

Nearly all respondents (99 per cent) wanted to receive SMS headlines from Pambazuka News.

Thirty per cent had witnessed domestic violence in varying degrees of incidence. While we were expecting high figures, we were astounded by the magnitude of the problem. Most incidences were not reported and all respondents were of the opinion that the UmNyango project could ameliorate the incidence of domestic violence through the dissemination of information, and allowing individuals to report incidents and to seek appropriate support. Of all the respondents interviewed, none indicated that they were actual victims of domestic violence. We feel that this is not a true reflection of the reality and that respondents deliberately denied being victims as they were embarrassed and/or fearful of intimidation, especially seeing that the interviews were conducted in the respondents' households. Due to financial constraints, we were unable to invite respondents to a neutral venue to conduct the interviews.

Thirty-three per cent of respondents (all women) reported that they had been illegally excluded from accessing and/or denied control of land. Respondents felt that the UmNyango project could assist in this lack of access through awareness raising via the SMS gateway and podcasting, and also through education and training.

Fifty-four per cent reported that they did not participate in governance in their communities due to the inaccessibility of relevant information, inaccessible local councillors and the cost of telephonic communications. In addition, civil society organisations were either weak or non-existent and therefore community members lacked the skills for advocacy, lobbying and campaigning.

Fifty-four per cent had experienced conflict in their communities, particularly around stock theft, land and politics, and 86 per cent felt that the UmNyango project provided a good opportunity for conflict resolution.

The majority of respondents felt that in regard to social capital, there were too few civil society organisations to meet their development needs. Those in existence were too weak to provide for these needs.

Other data collected included the demographic profile of each community, levels of education, types of occupation, household monthly income, types of transport used and safety and security issues.

The data collected confirmed our initial assumption that SMS technology is a tool the communities were willing to engage with for access to human rights information and for the reporting of human rights violations. We were also able to confirm the categories of human rights issues the project would focus on. It was with some relief that we were able to determine that the majority of community members owned a mobile phone and were able to send and receive an SMS via reliable networks within the five communities.

We then decided to target these five rural communities:

- Dondotha (KwaMbonambi)
- Limehill (Ladysmith)
- Muden (Greytown)
- Gcwensa (oThongathi)
- KwaDlangezwa (Empangeni).

This decision was based on the presence of a CLRDC paralegal advice office in the proximity of each target community, and its ability to provide paralegal services to clients referred to it by the partners. Another factor looked at was the presence of mobile phone networks. As shall be seen later, it was subsequently confirmed during the community survey that networks are an issue. The nearest of the communities to the city of Durban lies just over an hour's drive away with the furthest being at least three hours away. We were satisfied that the areas were deep flung rural areas. We were also satisfied that that the five communities did not have ready access to landlines, postal services, or to the internet. This was important if we were to test the feasibility of SMS and podcasting technology.

Registration of participants

In the immediate phase after the survey was completed we registered 161 community members in the five communities who were willing to participate in the project. Of these, 116 (72 per cent) were women and 45 (28 per cent) were men. Males were included as participants in the project for two reasons. Firstly, we were aware from the GenARDIS project that excluding them would cause gender conflict within the home and within the community. Although we had intended that at least 33 per cent of all participants be male, we had not excluded any males from participating. The youngest participant was 21 and the oldest 58, with most participants falling in the 30–40 age group.

Developing the SMS gateway and training

We needed to use an SMS gateway for two-way communication. This would allow us to send SMS information to participants, and participants to send information back to us. We accordingly needed to provide the appropriate training both to our partners and the participants.

We had chosen to use Clickatell's (www.clickatell.com) web-based Interactive Campaign Manager as our platform for the SMS gateway. This allows for two-way messaging across all mobile networks in South Africa. A five-digit central number was registered for us by Clickatell at no cost and the monthly rental of this number was also provided free of charge. The central number was allocated five keywords in IsiZulu, each representing one of the five categories of human rights information the project was focusing on. In this way, communities could elect who to send their reports and requests for information to. Partners, on the other hand, could identify which messages were sent for their specific attention. For example, if a participant wanted to report a matter pertaining to access to land, they would send their message to the central number and would precede the message with the keyword *umhlaba* meaning 'land' in IsiZulu. We also set up user profiles for each of the five partners and subscribed the participants to the system.

In order for the partners to send messages to the 161 participants, credits were bought and loaded onto the system. The system has an interface for this. Clickatell donated 12,000 credits as well as paying for the registration and rental of the central number.

Training manuals were developed for partners and communities. Eleven staff members from the five partner organisations were trained during a workshop and the 161 participants were trained in-field.

Production of messages

Partners produced lists of SMS information to be sent out in IsiZulu. These were tested by the partners for relevance through community workshops in-field, and amended in response to the results of the survey before being sent out.

Each partner was allocated a day in the week to send out their SMS messages between 10am and noon. Each partner sent out five unique messages every week for the period July–October 2007. The system limits the number of characters transmitted to 160. Most messages going out were more than the 160-character limit and so were concatenated (joined) by the system. In total, 300 messages were sent out to each of the 161 participants. The system therefore handled 48,300 outgoing messages. There were 207 incoming messages.

Partners were satisfied with the functionality of the SMS gateway established, which they also found to be user friendly. Ninety per cent of the messages sent by the partners were received by the participants. Those not receiving messages had either changed their sim cards or had their cell phones stolen or had lost them.

SMS transmission

Approximately 300 messages were transmitted by the partners. The specific categories of information sent out by each partner were:

- CPP: how rural communities can participate in local government, good governance, and policy and legislative processes
- DVAP: relevant provisions of the Domestic Violence Act and the Children's Rights Act and how they can be used to protect the rights of victims, Maintenance Act, information on counselling and legal support, gender equality clause in the constitution
- RWM: Labour Tenant Act, Extension of Security of Tenure Act, Communal Land Rights Act, Labour Relations Act, Employment Equity Act, Traditional Leadership and Governance Framework Act, right of women to inherit land, access and control of land by women, participation by women in traditional structures, counselling and legal support
- PDI: types of conflict, effects of conflict, avoiding conflict, resolving conflict, freedom of speech and association, cultural and religious freedoms, support for alternative dispute resolution services
- CLRDC: Unemployment Insurance Fund, social grants applications, pension funds, provident funds, estates of deceased people, compensation for occupational injuries and motor vehicle accidents, following-up on matters referred by the other UmNyango partners.

Only 207 messages were received by the partners from the participants. Of these, 70 per cent were sent by women. It would appear that participants were happy to receive messages raising their awareness but thereafter preferred to take any further action face-to-face via the paralegal advice offices.

All participants kept some sort of record on the messages they received. We distributed notebooks to most participants. Most participants transcribed the messages into the notebooks, while others preferred keeping them on their phones. We also targeted community development workers (CDWs) in each community, and they were instrumental in becoming what they call 'walking sources of information'. They carefully transcribed the information they received from each of the partners and advertised themselves as available to share this information with the communities. They indicated that they had had informal meetings, particularly with the youth, and that these discussions were very effective in raising their awareness. In addition to CDWs, most participants had shared the information they received with family members, friends and neighbours not registered or participating in the UmNyango project. Interestingly, many participants had also forwarded the messages to people in the contact lists on their phones. It is rather unfortunate that we did not make provision for assessing this roll-on effect, but the financial constraints did not allow for this.

Impact directly attributed to SMS

The survey and subsequent participant evaluations clearly showed that the technology chosen was easily accessible and user friendly, and that the messages received by the participants were in accordance with their needs.

There was a positive change in how the communities perceived the use of SMS technology and this implies that the project's intervention is now accorded higher priority than at the beginning of the project. However, the continuation of benefits to the communities is unlikely without further funding. We have looked at various alternatives but the use of SMS technology as a tool will always result in associated costs. This could be mitigated through 'no-charge' agreements with mobile networks, for example, but in the long term even this is not sustainable.

The project clearly showed that each of the five focus areas was relevant to the needs of the five communities that participated in the project. Importantly, though, the project demonstrated that while there was an overwhelming willingness by participants to receive SMS information on their human rights, they were not inclined either to request further information nor to report violations against them via SMS. Instead, there was a tendency to revert to local structures such as CLRDC's paralegal advice offices, which have a presence and a shared history in each of the five communities. This immediately points to a significant flaw in the design of the project. We ought to have included a mixture of communities in the project, some with advice offices and others where no back-up service was provided. This would have enabled us to analyse whether the presence of the advice offices had any influence on how participants engaged with the messages they received.

We have, however, been able to show that in the five communities the project had a marked impact on the work of the CLRDC paralegal advice offices on gender-based violence and women's preclusion from land. In the pre-live period (April–June 2007), approximately 179 women and 128 men attended 18 workshops facilitated by the local paralegal office. In the live period (July–September 2007) these numbers increased to 418 women and 316 men attending 22 workshops. As can be seen, the number of women and men attending workshops more than doubled. The paralegals determined during the course of the workshops they facilitated that the increase in participants was due to the project. To make sure that this was the case, we monitored workshop attendance in five other communities, where there are CLRDC advice offices, but where UmNyango was not operating. In these communities, there was practically no change in attendance levels.

We also monitored the number of cases opened by the advice offices. In the pre-live period, approximately 56 women and 16 men had opened cases relevant to the project focus at the advice offices. In the live period these numbers increased to 117 women and 19 men. More than twice the number of women were reporting cases during the live phase of the project. The increase in the number of women compared to that of men is significant, as most cases reported by women related to women's human rights – gender-based violence and access to and control of land.

Again, the paralegal offices confirmed that the cases were opened as UmNyango referrals. To make sure that this was the case we monitored cases opened at CLRDC advice offices in five other communities, where UmNyango was not operating. In these communities, again there was no discernable change in the number of cases opened.

The increase in numbers attending workshops and the increase in cases opened can be interpreted in two ways. First, it could be that the project raised awareness of participants to a level where they felt compelled to ask the paralegal for further information (activating the paralegals' facilitation of workshops), and also to file formal complaints for investigation by the paralegal. Second, it could be that the increase was due to more violations being perpetrated. The paralegals have confirmed that the former scenario is true.

Impact

Participation in local government

Although participation in local government was a primary concern of those participating in the project, SMS technology did not enhance their potential for this. In only one community was there some solid evidence to show that the project enhanced potential for participation, with local government now sharing their budgets and their integrated development plans with the community for comment. This was as a direct result of the project. While we acknowledge that it was the project that raised awareness levels, participants felt that they would have preferred the project to have focused on the establishment of an institutionalised forum where the community could interface directly with their local government councillors and officials. In conjunction with this, they would also have preferred to receive workshop-based training on lobbying and monitoring local government.

Reporting violence against women

We received very few requests for information and even fewer reports of gender-based violence. This is an indication that SMS technology is not a good vehicle for doing this. It would seem that the participants prefer receiving further information from the paralegal and in fact would also prefer reporting violations against them face-to-face with a trusted person such as the paralegal. It is worth noting that CLRDC places paralegals to work only in communities they themselves come from. This is due to a reluctance by community members to confide in anyone outside of their community.

Given this, and given the confidential nature of matters relating to gender-based violence, it is not surprising that women have chosen to approach the advice offices for a personal and face-to-face engagement. It would seem, then, that strengthening the capacity of the advice offices to receive complaints and provide counselling services for abused women might have had a greater impact than the SMS service. In addition, the project might also have had a greater impact by establishing official links with local police stations in order to build their awareness and capacity to deal with complaints about gender-based violence. This might have even precipitated the establishment of specialised advice desks located within the police station.

Women's access to land

The results relating to women's preclusion from access to and control of land echo those relating to gender-based violence. We might have seen a greater impact had we provided for possible solutions for systemic problems. For example, traditional authorities are responsible for land allocation, control and use, and for dispute resolution. Had the project focused on interventions that might have sensitised traditional authorities to respond in a more equitable fashion in regard to the needs of women, we might have seen a greater impact.

Reporting of political tensions

In the area of conflict, once more, the results do not show that the project had an impact. This is partly explained by the fact that there was not any significant political violence during the live phase of the project. However, given the trends on impact already discussed above, we are not confident that the facility provided by the project would have been effectively utilised had any political conflict taken place. The project might have had a greater impact had we built the capacity of the paralegals and a group of community members to monitor and resolve disputes and report on political conflict.

Access to justice

The project had its greatest impact as a tool to complement the existing activity of the CLRDC paralegal advice offices. CLRDC was responsible for access to justice via their advice offices located in each of the five rural communities. We have already shown how the project contributed to greater attendances at workshops and enhanced the reporting of gender-based violence and gender-based land discrimination. As such, we can conclude that the project had a very important function in providing supplementary information to participants in order for them to take up issues directly with the advice offices.

This indicates that the project ought to have strengthened the capacity of the advice offices to more effectively handle matters being reported to them. Given the spread of their advice offices and ever dwindling funding, CLRDC has been unable to provide update training to their existing paralegals. The paralegals also lack back-up legal services from lawyers. Both are significant factors, as not only are the paralegals not up-to-date with legal developments, but also they have no recourse for litigious matters that are referred to them by the communities. We have already alluded to statistics proving that the project led to more awareness raising via workshops and to more complaints lodged. The lack of update training for paralegals will certainly have a negative impact on raising the awareness of the communities' human rights. In regard to the lack of access to lawyers, it is admirable that so many more cases have been reported as a consequence of the project, but what next? The paralegals do not have the capacity to counsel victims of gender-based violence, nor conciliate, mediate or arbitrate either over political conflict, or on issues of women's preclusion from access to and control of land. Worse still, without access to lawyers who might litigate on their behalf, the effect is that in cases where a matter is deemed litigious, no further action can be taken. In this regard, the project would have had a greater impact if funds were made available for the solicitation of pro bono or contingency arrangements with local lawyers, or establishing back-up legal services with state legal aid structures.

Sustainability

As far as sustainability is concerned, using SMS technology is prohibitively expensive, unless long-term agreements can be concluded with networks or they can be subsidised by local businesses advertising on the SMS messages transmitted. We disbursed approximately ZAR 37,000 for the transmission of about 48,300 messages. On the other hand, the communities are poverty stricken and we had to purchase airtime for them (approximately ZAR 4,000) to send messages to the partners. It is interesting to note that Indiba-Africa Development Alliance (IADA) based in Durban, KZN, is currently developing a human rights information website on the .mobi domain. This website, specifically designed for browsing by mobile phones, uses new and award-winning technology developed in KZN to minimise the cost of mobile browsing. The site is currently in development and can be accessed at www.indiba-africa.mobi.

Conclusion

We examined whether SMS technology could be used as an effective tool to enhance political participation and to enable women both to report on and organise around domestic violence and land exclusions. However, our pilot project suggests that this is fraught with problems (especially given that this was not demand-driven by the communities involved), because SMS technology is an expensive method of communicating. However, we have demonstrated that SMS technology is an important supplementary information tool and this has been borne out by the facilitation of workshops and by the opening of cases with the advice offices.

Indeed, had we used the funds for supporting women in other ways to organise and seek redress, the outcome would have been more positive than spending the effort and resources in setting up, administering and sending SMS messages. Our recommendation would be that the use of SMS might at best be used as a complement to social organising rather than as the central part. We recognise that this conclusion may not be very popular with those who want to promote the use of SMS, and that we may be perceived as going against the current fashion which regards mobile phone technology as 'sexy'. However, this pilot study does demonstrate that there is no substitute for human social and political organising, and technical tools are just that – tools. And to be effective in achieving social justice, the right tools need to be used for the right purpose. This pilot project has allowed us to learn these lessons empirically, and for that we are grateful to those who supported the project.

7

Kubatana in Zimbabwe: mobile phones for advocacy

Amanda Atwood

Background

Since 2000, Zimbabwe has experienced a growing political and economic crisis. Zimbabwe's media environment has become increasingly closed as political tensions have increased. Independent newspapers have been shut down. Freelance and independent journalists routinely face harassment. Repressive legislation such as the Access to Information and Protection of Privacy Act (AIPPA) and the Broadcasting Services Act (BSA) have further challenged the operations of any independent media house. Fees gazetted in January 2009 make operating as a freelance journalist for a foreign media house in Zimbabwe prohibitively expensive.[1] Submissions by the Media Monitoring project of Zimbabwe (MMPZ) to the African Charter on Human and Peoples' Rights session in May 2008[2] outline many of these obstacles. The June 2008 reports by the International Federation of Journalists (IFJ),[3] and International Freedom of Expression exchange (IFEX)[4] further explore the conditions faced by journalists trying to operate independently in Zimbabwe.

Zimbabwe's economic crisis, framed by crippling inflation, has restricted people's access to information throwing it, according to an article by *The Times* (UK) journalist Jan Raath, into the 'dark ages'.[5] The state-run daily and weekly newspapers, radio stations and television stations are widely acknowledged to be laden with bias and propaganda. The few remaining independent weekly newspapers are out of reach of much of the population because of cost and the limitations placed on their distribution by the Mugabe government: rural areas are controlled by the ruling party making the delivery of independent information difficult.

A small number of elite Zimbabweans can afford Multichoice DSTV packages from South Africa. Wiztech decoders, which bring in South African Broadcasting Corporation channels, Botswana TV and ETV, are growing in popularity, as a more affordable satellite TV option, but their coverage of Zimbabwe is limited. SW Radio Africa, Voice of America Studio 7 and Radio Voice of the People try to address the information vacuum through providing evening short-wave radio broadcasts but they are often jammed or have a poor signal. The high unemployment rates in Zimbabwe mean that fewer and fewer people can access the internet, or even email, via the workplace. Power shortages and a broader lack of resources have reduced the potential of internet access at universities and polytechnics. Thus, Zimbabweans' options for news about their own country are largely limited to the state media. Independent information initiatives are treated with suspicion with labels such as 'pirate radio stations' or 'underground newspapers' attached to them.

The net result of this information void is despair and fear. Repressive governments leverage this to abuse their power and manipulate the citizenry.

Kubatana – an information success story

Founded in 2001, the Kubatana Trust of Zimbabwe aggregates civil society information and shares it with subscribers via the internet, email, SMS and print publications. Kubatana is also a community of activists, sharing information, ideas and inspiration to encourage and create a new Zimbabwe. Kubatana is defined by its constant flow of information – both drawing it in to include in the archive, and actively sending it back out again to share with others.

The engine of Kubatana is its internet library of over 15,500 statements by civil society organisations, news articles, and reports. Information is sorted by date, issue and topical indexes, providing an easy-to-search resource for journalists, researchers, activists and others seeking to know more about the situation in

Zimbabwe. Fact sheets for local NGOs make contact information and background details available in a regularly updated directory giving organisations an online profile without them having to create or maintain their own websites.

Knowing that many Zimbabweans can access their email more easily than they can surf the internet, Kubatana sends out regular email newsletters sharing highlighted content with over 7,500 subscribers, most of whom are based in Zimbabwe. The newsletters also contain announcements about upcoming public meetings, workshops, fellowships and vacancies in the NGO sector.

The Kubatana community blog (http://kubatanablogs.net/kubatana/) provides a space for more personal and anecdotal writing from over 20 Zimbabwean writers. Through the comments section it also opens up conversation and debate, further increasing the space for ordinary voices to be heard and publicly recognised. These informal pieces provide a much needed window into daily life in Zimbabwe. International media houses such as the BBC, CNN, Sky and the *New York Times* have looked to the Kubatana community blog for a range of opinion and vox pops from Zimbabweans.

Our work with mobile phones

While barely 5 per cent of Zimbabweans have access to the internet or email there are over 2 million mobile phone contracts for the country's 11 million people. This represents a penetration rate of roughly 20 per cent. Recognising these factors, Kubatana launched an SMS-based information service in 2007.

SMS reaches people immediately and directly, wherever they are. A text message lands on your phone, in your pocket or your handbag and you read it. If you're with other people, you often share what the message says with them. You can save a message on your phone and take it home to share with your family or friends later. The character constraints on an SMS mean that the messages are invariably short, specific and direct. These factors mean that, particularly in an information-starved oral culture such as Zimbabwe, text messages are shared by far more than the direct recipients. In a hostile political environment text messaging provides a safer way of receiving information.

Kubatana uses SMS to tell subscribers about public events or other upcoming meetings, encourage specific advocacy actions, offer print materials or videos via post, or to share news flashes such as election results. We also use SMS to ask subscribers for their thoughts and suggestions about current events. To provide an even wider avenue for dialogue we share feedback from subscribers in our blogs or email newsletters. Examples of this integration and amplification can be found at:

- Kara Rowland, 'Mobile technology a lifeline, a source of news and inspiration', http://www.gopachy.com/forum/comments.php?DiscussionID=21417Ndesanjo Macha, 'Zimbabwe: Using New Technologies to Fight for Democracy', http://globalvoicesonline.org/2008/05/06/zimbabwe-using-new-technologies-to-fight-for-democracy
- Ken Banks, 'Kubatana reaches out with FrontlineSMS in Zimbabwe', http://www.blogspot.kiwanja.net/2008/04/kubatana-reaches-out-with-frontlinesms.html
- New Tactics for Human Rights, 'Kubatana in Zimbabwe using mobile phones tactic!', http://www.newtactics.org/blog/kantin/kubatana-zimbabwe-using-mobile-phones-tactic
- Corinne Ramey and Katrin Verclas, MobileActive, 'SMS as alternative media in elections', http://mobileactive.org/sms-alternative-media-elections.

Kubatana also provides creative and technical SMS support to a variety of civil society organisations, helping them to harness the power of new media to communicate with often diverse geographical communities.

Two-way communication is key

At Kubatana, information campaigns are viewed as cyclic, with key objectives being to elicit feedback from subscribers and to recruit more subscribers with each communication. We view two-way communication as essential. Kubatana facilitates the expression of citizens' voices in Zimbabwe's hostile media environment. This makes our work more difficult and presents some risk to those who choose to communicate with us.

When we first started our SMS service, we invited our email newsletter subscribers to join and to encourage their friends to subscribe as well. The objective was to use SMS to share information with people who didn't necessarily have email so we also bought advertising space in the local press. Because the daily newspaper, *The Herald*, is state run, it often refuses to publish adverts that it deems too overtly 'political' or human rights related. To get around this problem and to make the most of our advertising budget, we ran a series of text-based classified adverts which we placed in the vacancies and personals sections. *The Herald* is largely read for its classifieds so we knew our target audience would see our adverts.

As a result of this advertising our subscriber list grew to over 1,000 by March 2008. Having gained this initial core of subscribers, word of mouth helped our SMS membership really take off. As of October 2009, it stood at over 7,500, and we get over 200 new subscribers per month, without further advertising.

Establishing a genuinely two-way communication service takes time, thoughtfulness and thoroughness. When we send messages out to our subscribers, we are careful always to include a way that they can get back to us. We keep our SMS receive console (see below) on at all times, so that we can always receive replies. Every day we process these replies: regularly adding new subscribers or, less frequently, removing people at their request (usually because they are leaving the country or selling their line); posting or emailing information that has been requested; and sharing with others messages we've received, in order to further broaden the reach of information.

The messages we receive from subscribers mirror the richness and diversity of Zimbabwe's public. Typically, people text us to respond to a question from us (What do you think about negotiations, or a stay away, or dollarisation?) or to request something we have offered (a DVD or report or article). But each week there are also dozens of messages from people just communicating – reporting if they have seen an unusual police or army presence in their area, asking where they can go for cholera treatment or how to get a scholarship for their child, or requesting an update on news events like the post-election negotiations over the formation of the transitional government and parliament.

Messages to and from subscribers peak during important national events, such as the March 2008 harmonised election and the June 2008 presidential run-off election. A look at the difference in content and feeling from these two periods gives a good indication of the difference in Zimbabweans' attitudes more generally during these two events. In March and April, the messages we received from subscribers focused around wanting to know where to vote, and then (particularly as the Zimbabwe Electoral Commission delayed its announcements) what the election results were. As we texted people results, they increasingly responded with both frustration and determination.

> It is clear they are already rigging. *Pasina izvozvo ZANU haihwinhi*. We need to plan way forward not *kuenda kucourt kwavo*. [Zanu PF won't win. We need to plan our way forward, not go back and challenge this election in court.][6]

> Why are the election results taking forever to be announced? We hope they don't want to employ some dirty tricks. The people of Zimbabwe wont accept any such rubbish. Enough is enough. The people have spoken and their word should be honoured.

> What criteria are they using *kuti paite madraw* [that the results are a tie]. If they are busy rigging tell them that I'm prepared to die 4 this country![7]

The Movement for Democratic Change (MDC) pulled out of the June 2008 presidential run-off election a week before it was scheduled. The messages we received from our subscribers during this period reflected people's disbelief that Mugabe would go ahead with the 'election' without the MDC. When the run-off 'results' were announced, these messages expressed people's rejection of what they saw as Mugabe hijacking the process.

> This is not any election *vapererwa nyikahaisiyavo mdc inotongachete*. [Zanu PF is finished – they don't own the country. MDC must govern.]

> What's happening is typical of zanu pf, filthy lying. I think this so called runoff was meant 2 give them a higher advantage at neg. tables saying they won last.

> Presidential run off it took a month and a half to announce false results now it only took less than a day to announce the so called win food for thought.[8]

At Kubatana, we have found the time spent building a community – not just a one-way information service – to be rewarding and worthwhile. In Zimbabwe, many organisations put adverts in the newspaper without including their contact information. Others distribute flyers anonymously, without even naming the organisation behind the action. Whilst this is an understandable reaction to the state crackdown on independent voices, it is also self-censorship. For the past eight years, Kubatana has put its name to its messages and given people a way to contact it. By consistently inviting Zimbabweans to share their thoughts with us, and sharing this feedback with our network and other subscribers, we have built our credibility with a community that trusts us, is happy to receive the information we provide, and ready to respond to us with their thoughts and ideas.

Given Zimbabwe's political environment, and the high levels of fear many experience, this trust is particularly important to us. Many people perceive being 'political' – or even simply communicating their ideas and frustrations openly – as risky. And yet, we have a ready exchange of thoughts and suggestions from people we have never met. We have been impressed by the large number of people who communicate with us directly, sharing their thoughts and opinions and using their own name, email address, postal address and/or mobile number.

Mobile phone campaigning

We were first turned onto the idea of SMS campaigning through FrontlineSMS. Established by Ken Banks, FrontlineSMS enables organisations to send bulk text messages without needing internet access. Instead, you take a small sim card modem, or even certain mobile phone handsets, slot your sim card into it, plug the modem into the computer, and let FrontlineSMS's intuitive GUI guide you through sending and receiving text messages.

Because of Zimbabwe's network congestion issues, and the large size of our mailing list, FrontlineSMS is no longer an efficient solution for our outgoing messages. Instead, we send messages using an online bulk SMS gateway called Clickatell. We set our message-sending ID to our local Zimbabwean mobile number.

We then use FrontlineSMS, and the sim card for our

Zimbabwean mobile number, to receive messages. The application is small enough that it can be left to run in the background while the computer is used for other things.

Any text messages that are sent to the Kubatana mobile number are captured into a text file, which can then be imported into a spreadsheet so that the comments and new subscriptions to our mobile information service can easily be sorted with the numbers they have come from. Each day, we take the text file of received messages that FrontlineSMS has created for us, and process these – adding new subscribers, responding to requests, or sharing feedback as and where appropriate.

Our SMS messages can be divided into several general categories – elections, news and information, inspiration, activism, feedback and access to information.

Elections

During the 2008 elections in Zimbabwe we kept our subscribers informed of the parliamentary and senate results, and the gender breakdown of these seats. As the election results slowly trickled out, our timely text message service kept people informed in the face of a general media blackout.

> Kubatana! Some poll stations asking foreign borns for renunciation certificates. This is NOT a requirement. Call Zim Lawyers to assist – 091278995 / 04251468

> Kubatana! Results have not been officially announced yet. The MDC has claimed victory based on preliminary counts – majorities in HRE, Mash Central and Masvingo

> Kubatana! Final senate results ZPF 30, MDC(MT) 24, MDC(AM) 6. Twenty out of sixty senators are women.

We also supported a text message-based voters' roll inquiry service during the June presidential run-off election. Since 2000, Zimbabwe's changing legislation has disenfranchised many Zimbabweans. But the disorganised state of the voters' roll means that many people who thought they were disenfranchised have either re-registered elsewhere, or are still on the roll. At the same time, electoral laws now require ward-based voting – you have to cast your ballot at a polling station in the ward where you are registered. However, many people don't remember which ward they registered in. Updating this information each time you move is difficult and time consuming, and includes a rigorous proof of residence process – which many renters, in particular, cannot meet. Also, polling stations often change between elections – so the place where you voted in the last election might not even be a polling station this time around. Going to the registrar's office to check whether you're on the roll, and where you can vote, is also time consuming and inconvenient to many people.

After years of requesting an electronic version of the voters' roll, the opposition Movement for Democratic Change was finally granted its wish. However, rather than being given the roll in a spreadsheet or text file format, it was given the voters' roll as a series of jpeg images. A technical team then OCR-scanned these jpegs, cross checked them for errors, and eventually created a database of the voters' roll for the entire country, including name, ID number, constituency and ward.

Working with this database, we contracted a developer to help create an SMS-based service, enabling users to query the database. Zimbabweans sent a text message to a local number, and were sent a reply telling them whether they were on the voters' roll, in which ward and which constituency. The query could also distinguish valid ID numbers from invalid ones – giving users the chance to resubmit their query if they had mistyped their ID number. If a valid ID number was found not to be on the voters' roll, the user was sent a reply with the contact number of a help centre, where they could follow it up.

News and information

SMS lends itself to communicating short news headlines. Kubatana uses text messages to alert people to breaking news events, such as the death of Levy Mwanawasa or the signing of the Global Political Agreement between the three major political parties in Zimbabwe.

Inspiration

Periodically, we send inspirational quotations to our subscribers in an effort to lift their spirits and encourage participation.

Kubatana! If we want to climb out of the hole that we are in, it is a job for all the people. Chinua Achebe. <VOTE!>

Kubatana! Hope is like a path in the country; there was never a path but when many people walk on it, the path comes into existence.

Kubatana! Against brute force and injustice the people will have the last word. That of victory. Che Guevara

Activism

Kubatana engages SMS to encourage participation in targeted activism. Given the constraints of text messages, SMS is not an effective method for communicating details of a campaign in full. However, it is sufficient to spark people to action around an issue they are already concerned about, or to direct people to participate in a specific action.

Kubatana! Email Zimbabwe Electoral Commission (zecpr@gta. gov.zw) or phone them 04 781903 and complain about unacceptable delays in announcement of results.

Feedback

Drawing on our commitment to two-way communication we often seek feedback from our subscribers via SMS. We regularly receive hundreds of replies to these requests.

Kubatana! No senate results as at 5.20 pm. What changes do YOU want in a free Zim? Let's inspire each other. Want to know what others say? SMS us your email addr.

Kubatana! The MDC has called for a strike from 15 April until the pres election results are announced. Is your workplace closed tomorrow? <Defend your vote!>

Kubatana! The High Court today refused to order immediate release of the pres results & dismissed the MDC application with costs. How should the nation respond?

In that heady first week of April 2008, when a new government in Zimbabwe seemed imminent, we used SMS to ask people what they wanted to change in a new Zimbabwe. We received replies from over 300 different people with a diverse and inspirational range of large and small dreams. Many people wrote in wanting to see repressive legislation such as the Public Order and Security Act (POSA) and AIPPA repealed, and wanting a new constitution. Some wrote in about the economy, inflation, healthcare, education and access to sanitary ware. These responses from ordinary Zimbabweans form a draft people's charter. We look forward to using this experience to compile and publish a booklet of ideas, facts, and tips which will be distributed to thousands of Zimbabweans with resource information encouraging them to get involved in small steps to create the new Zimbabwe they want. Read some of these comments at http://kubatanablogs.net/kubatana/?p=474

Read other examples of text responses at:

- Interparty talks – Zimbabweans speak out,
  http://kubatanablogs.net/kubatana/?p=718
- MDC election pull out – Zimbabweans speak out,
  http://kubatanablogs.net/kubatana/?p=655
- We are the ones the run off is waiting for,
  http://kubatanablogs.net/kubatana/?p=589
- GNU: Sell out or solution? Zimbabweans speak out,
  http://kubatanablogs.net/kubatana/?p=576
- Text messages for change,
  http://kubatanablogs.net/kubatana/?p=451
- Get out the mobile vote,
  http://kubatanablogs.net/kubatana/?p=417
- National stay away – Zimbabweans speak out,
  http://kubatanablogs.net/kubatana/?p=201

Access to information

Kubatana uses SMS to make a variety of information more accessible to our subscribers. For example, when the Global Political Agreement was signed between the three major political parties in Zimbabwe, we offered to post it or email it to subscribers. We received over 200 requests for it by email, and over 300 requests for post – a useful reminder of how SMS can reach people who do not have internet access.

In another example, the Solidarity Peace Trust (SPT) regularly produces short DVDs about current issues, such as starvation, cholera and election violence. We alert our SMS subscribers that we have these DVDs available, and they text us their postal address to request that we send them to them. This facilitates a nationwide dissemination of information materials ordinarily hard to achieve because of the difficulty in distributing information in areas hostile to civil society organisations.

Freedom Fone – extending mobile activism

Beyond our SMS information service, Kubatana is excited about its most recent initiative, Freedom Fone. The idea for Freedom Fone came to Brenda Burrell, Kubatana's technical director, at MobileActive 2005. A winner of the 2008 Knight News Challenge, Freedom Fone is still in the initial stages of development.

Freedom Fone takes advantage of the affordability and increasing popularity of the mobile phone. It has the potential to provide current, relevant news and information to a range of people – without the access constraints of email or the internet. In addition, Freedom Fone opens up the potential to say much more than one can with the 160 character constraints of SMS.

It is a new technology that will enable communities to leverage the growing popularity of mobile phones, and the personal, on-demand capacity they have to provide information to users. It marries this with citizen radio-style programming, allowing organisations to create content that the public can access in their own time by listening to short audio files on their phone.

Audio files are stored by Freedom Fone in a content management system (CMS), that is updated through a simple-to-use browser interface. These audio clips populate an interactive voice response (IVR) menu through which callers can navigate for information. IVR menus are the series of prompts and content you encounter when, for example, you phone a large company and an automated voice instructs you to 'Press 1 for sales, 2 for the help desk, 3 for customer care' and so forth.

Freedom Fone will enable organisations to create exciting audio information magazines. Because all the files, from the core content through to the user menu prompts, can be created by the organisation, Freedom Fone can be deployed in any language – or even more than one language – through a single phone number.

Individuals can contribute questions, content and feedback by leaving voice messages via the IVR interface. Freedom Fone can be operated as a collective, with different groups managing different channels (IVR menu options) of information from the same installation.

Freedom Fone is network agnostic and can work easily and happily with mobiles and landlines. Where possible, this means it can even connect to hunting lines, or high capacity (E1 or T1) landlines, so that a single phone number can carry multiple concurrent calls. In countries where voice over internet protocol (VoIP) is available, organisations can also scale the product up again by having just one phone number which 30 (or possibly more) users can dial into at the same time.

This technology can be used in a 'cost free to caller' context – where users could either dial a toll-free number to access the service or leave a missed call, effectively 'tickling' a number that records the user's phone number and calls them back, connecting them to the IVR menu content. In a 'low cost to caller' context, users can SMS in for a call back. Or one person can send a text message which requests a call back at a specific time, or even to a friend or family member on a different mobile number or a landline.

There are no geographical or community size limitations to the implementation of Freedom Fone. The interface facilitates frequently updated, short-segment audio programming. It removes the technical challenge of hosting and setting up the back end, allowing users to concentrate on content.

Information in the system will be updated continuously and will be available to callers 24 hours a day, overcoming the hurdles of literacy, printing, distribution and time delays which print-based initiatives often encounter. The simple nature of the user interface, the open nature of telecommunications and the low equipment requirements of the system make it a more affordable and accessible option than starting a radio station or buying an hour of radio time each week to communicate an organisation's message.

Elements used by Freedom Fone are not new, but no one else has developed non-commercial, user-friendly, dial-up, radio-on-demand technology for the non-profit sector which could enable

NGOs and service organisations to easily upload short-segment audio content that can be accessed directly through the telephones of small-scale farmers and other constituencies. Global Voices' Ethan Zuckerman said recently that it was 'surprising that there hasn't been more work done making interactive voice response systems usable for development purposes'.[9] Freedom Fone provides exactly that. The intuitive convergence of radio and mobile phones makes the project innovative and globally relevant.

We launched the first public deployment of Freedom Fone at the Association for Women's Rights in Development (AWID) 2008 Forum in Cape Town.[10] We have secured funding for extensive development and deployment of this service both in Zimbabwe and the region, and we plan to develop call-in information services around issues such as HIV/AIDS, elections, and small-scale farmer support.

Other uses of Freedom Fone could include:

- Youth/sexual health – research indicates individuals provided with information on HIV are most likely to positively alter their behaviour
- Community radio stations – extending audio programming to be available as dial-up information; especially useful where the application procedure for broadcasting licences is expensive or difficult
- Get out the vote/voter education – providing information on polling stations as well as facilitating feedback from citizens detailing electoral irregularities
- Displaced/vulnerable groups, such as commercial sex workers or immigrants – making essential information available and building community.

At the time of going to publication, we have engaged a development team to further develop the software. We hope the beta version will be running by November 2009 and a more fully featured version by April 2010. We will then be looking for organisations with strong communications, information and technical capacity, with whom we can partner for targeted deployments of Freedom Fone.

We are also currently working on local deployments of Freedom Fone. These will pose many challenges, particularly in connecting the Freedom Fone server to a functioning telephony system locally (such as VoIP, GSM or landline). All of these options face constraints of power and require special configurations to function with the server.

Previously, one of our greatest concerns for deploying Freedom Fone in Zimbabwe was network congestion. Zimbabwe's cell phone networks were oversubscribed. Making a call typically entailed at least a dozen unsuccessful attempts, and messages were often received hours after they were sent.

With dollarisation (see section on limitations, below), network congestion may ease. But it also means much greater cost hurdles for users. Thus, we look forward to developing a product model that is able to subsidise some portion of users in order to make the service more accessible to poor communities. We are also looking to explore the multi-tenant, hosted version of Freedom Fone that allows organisations to share overheads, thus reducing their own administrative costs and increasing the likelihood of finding advertising revenue or corporate sponsorship that is able to subsidise programme and caller costs. In July 2009, Kubatana launched Inzwa, a pilot deployment of our audio magazine featuring a daily headline service and information on activism, culture, jobs and opportunities, which is updated weekly. Find out more about Inzwa at http://www.kubatana.net/html/archive/archinzwa_index.asp.

Find out more about Freedom Fone at:

- 'Dialling for information and news', Digital Planet, BBC News – http://news.bbc.co.uk/2/hi/technology/7785847.stm
- Ramey, C., 'MobileActive07 Preview! Mobiles as alternative media in Zimbabwe', MobileActive, http://mobileactive.org/mobileactive07-preview-m.

Limits to SMS and mobile advocacy

For Zimbabweans, mobile phones provide a more accessible form of communication than email or the internet, but mobile phone usage in Zimbabwe is lower than the continental rate of 30.4 per cent.[11] This is largely because of Zimbabwe's economic decline since 2000, just as mobile phones were becoming more affordable and commonplace elsewhere. Before January 2009, when the mobile phone network operators were licensed to price and sell their services in US dollars, new pre-paid and contract sim cards were very difficult to get from the mobile phone companies themselves. On the street or from a resale shop the going price for a new or used pre-paid line was around US$100.[12] Dollarisation may help the mobile companies stay afloat, and bring sim cards back into the formal market. But the current gazetted formal market prices are still much higher than regional averages. A pre-paid line now costs US$30 from Econet Wireless, Zimbabwe's strongest mobile phone company. Payment must be in foreign currency – and the company won't accept notes that look too crumpled or dirty. Getting a contract line means showing pay slips and bank statements that demonstrate earnings over US$700 per month (in foreign currency). Tariffs are charged in US dollars – and again can only be paid in foreign currency. At the beginning of 2009, costs were over US$0.30 per minute to phone, and over US$0.15 per text message – again much higher than the regional average.

In part, these high tariffs are a response to the fact that for the past several years the mobile phone operators were price-controlled to rates that were unsustainably low. These companies have run at a loss for years, and network maintenance and service has suffered for it, with congestion being the norm. Initially it was anticipated that once the companies recovered some of their costs, these prices would go down, given the pressure on them to align with the regional costing structure. Indeed, by September 2009 these costs were down to around US$.09 per text message and US$0.25 per minute to phone. But these costs remain high for the majority of Zimbabweans, who are unemployed and on a low-income.

In the past, we have observed how many people share the same phone – for example, we can receive several different opinions on the same issue from the same number in a day. Or we receive multiple requests to send material to different names and addresses, all coming from the same mobile number. These addresses are typically from schools or growth points in rural Zimbabwe. If mobile phone tariffs had remained as high as they were at the beginning of the year, we would likely have seen a decline in feedback from our members generally (as they prioritise other spending) and an increase in the frequency with which multiple messages or requests are sent in one text. Encouragingly, we continue to receive a high volume of feedback from our subscribers via SMS, and this two-way communications channel remains vibrant.

These rising costs – and the dramatically increased cost of living in Zimbabwe in general as the country has dollarised – will also impact on Kubatana's work. Because of our commitment to making information accessible to people who otherwise wouldn't get it, and given our desire to promote participation and civic engagement, we have been reluctant to charge for our services. Beyond the cost of their own access to the phone or computer, people do not pay to receive SMS messages from us, to receive our email newsletters, or to view our online library. We did, however, require users to cover the cost of their calls to Inzwa. In part, we wanted to measure how people would value the service, and in part we know that, whilst we might be able to fundraise to offer free calls for a specific timeframe or around a particular event, this is not a sustainable business model in the long term. Kubatana depends heavily on technical, material, creative and intellectual resources, all of which cost money. Thus, we are continuously challenged to find ways to become more financially sustainable.

Conclusion

A 2008 report, 'Limits on press freedom and regime support',[13] finds that 'state restrictions over news broadcasting can often achieve their intended effect' (p. 3), namely to 'suppress dissent (against) and mobilise support' (p. 4) for the ruling power. This means that creative, innovative approaches that make information more accessible to ordinary people can both confront state propaganda and make independent thinking and action more possible.

The growing presence of mobile phones makes them a valuable communication tool. In addition, mobiles offer potential as access equalisers. Mobile phones cross gender, class and social divides more effectively than satellite television, the internet and independent newspapers. We have found women to be more likely to own or have access to a mobile phone than to own or have access to a computer. The learning curve, and the resistance to learning a new technology, is much smaller with a mobile phone than with a computer, further equalising access. In terms of security, it can be unsafe or inconvenient for a woman to visit an internet café at night, after work or after her chores are done. But she always has a mobile phone on her. In terms of cost, it can be expensive to take transport to an internet café, and expensive to surf for 15 minutes at a time, so a mobile phone is an important medium for receiving information. Similarly, low-income and informal-sector workers often own a mobile phone, or live with someone who does. But it is uncommon for this group to have internet access or to be computer literate. Thus, the more information that can be provided via the mobile phone, the more the access to this information is extended and levelled.

As Kubatana looks ahead, we are looking forward to using Freedom Fone ourselves, and to sharing it with other organisations, in order to move activism and information out of the more exclusive space of the internet, and towards a more accessible, phone-based information service.

Notes

1. Local journalists working for a foreign media organisation must pay US$1,000 for an application and US$3,000 for accreditation for one year. See: (2009)'MIC pegs prohibitive registration fees', Radio VOP, 5 January, http://www.radiovop.com/index.php?option=com_content&task=view&id=488 3&Itemid=171, accessed 6 January 2009; (2009)'Journalists to pay through the nose', *The Zimbabwe Times*, 5 January, http://www.thezimbabwetimes.com/?p=9568, accessed 6 January 2009.
2. Moyo, B. (2008) 'No change in restrictive media landscape in Zim since last ACHPR session in May 2008', *Media Monitoring project Zimbabwe (MMPZ)*, 13 November, http://www.kubatana.net/html/archive/media/081113mmpz.asp?sector=MEDIA, accessed 18 December 2008.
3. IFJ (2008) 'Against the odds: Covering Zimbabwe in a climate of fear and physical danger', International Federation of Journalists (IFJ), 13 June, http://www.kubatana.net/html/archive/media/080613ifj.asp?sector=MEDI, accessed 18 September 2009.
4. IFEX (2008) 'Worst time for journalists in country's history', IFEX, 24 June, http://www.kubatana.net/html/archive/media/080624ifex.asp?sector=MEDIA, accessed 18 December 2008.
5. Raath, J. (2008) 'Economic crisis throws Zimbabwe into "information dark age"', *Monsters and Critics*, 7 October, http://www.kubatana.net/html/archive/media/081007mc.asp?sector=MEDIA, accessed 18 December 2008.

6. Read more at http://kubatanablogs.net/kubatana/?p=417, accessed 27 May 2009.

7. Ibid.

8. Text messages received 28 June 2008.

9. Zuckerman E. 'Delivering Ethiopian teff via Czech taxi?', http://www.ethanzuckerman.com/blog/2007/10/13/delivering-ethiopian-teff-via-czech-taxi/, accessed 31 August 2009.

10. Kubatana.net. 'Freedom Fone - Direct from AWID Forum 2008', http://www.kubatana.net/html/archive/women/081203kub.asp?sector=WOMEN, accessed 31 August 2009.

11. Hersman, E. (2008) '2007 African mobile phone statistics', 'White African' blog, 1 August, http://whiteafrican.com/2008/08/01/2007-african-mobile-phone-statistics/, accessed 21 January, 2009.

12. Contrast this with neighbouring South Africa, where one can get a new pre-paid line for ZAR1-5 – around US$0.10–0.50.

13. Norris, P. and Inglehart, R. (2008) 'Limits on press freedom and regime support', Harvard-World Bank Workshop paper 4.3 in *The Role of the News Media in the Governance Reform Agenda*, http://ksghome.harvard.edu/~pnorris/Conference/Conference%20papers/Limits_press_freedom_Norris_Inglehart.pdf, accessed 18 December 2008.

8

Women in Uganda: mobile activism for networking and advocacy

Berna Ngolobe

Introduction

ICT presents unique and timely opportunities for women and girls. It promises better economic prospects, fuller political participation, communication with the outside world, easy access to information, and an enhanced ability to acquire education and skills and to transcend social restrictions.

However, use of ICT continues to be governed by power relations whereby women frequently experience relative disadvantage. Women's lower levels of literacy and education relative to men, as well as negative attitudes towards girls' achievement in science and mathematics, contribute to the gender dimension of the digital divide. In addition, women have a lower degree of economic security than men and face gender-related constraints on their time and mobility. They are therefore less likely than men to access, use and participate in shaping the course of ICT. In Uganda women's awareness and usage of ICT is nearly three times less than that of men.[1]

Amid such inequality the Women of Uganda Network (WOUGNET) has directed its efforts to promoting and supporting the use of ICT by women and women's organisations in Uganda so that they can take advantage of the opportunities presented by ICT in order to address national and local problems of sustainable development. WOUGNET's activities are aimed at increasing ICT access and application, and influencing the formulation and implementation of gender sensitive ICT policies and programmes. Improvements in these areas are expected to result in increased availability and improved access to timely and relevant information. Activities are undertaken from a gender perspective, with particular emphasis on the needs and concerns of women and women's organisations in Uganda.

ICT and empowering women

Information sharing, dissemination and exchange

ICT has enabled women to share and exchange information on various themes by using email, SMS, listserves, online newsletters, radios, websites and other social networking tools.

For example 'e-agriculture' is increasingly being used to improve agricultural production. E-agricultural initiatives have played a key role in addressing the information gap to enable women, as the main contributors to the agricultural sector, to improve their productivity. Women and rural communities are able to access information on improving the quality of their products, acquiring improved seeds and crop varieties, information on where they can obtain materials and equipment, disease and pest control, soil management and conservation, and how to improve their production skills.

> E-agriculture is an emerging field comprising the enhancement of agriculture and rural development through improved information exchange, communication and learning processes, based on the use of internet and other digital technologies.[2]

In Uganda, the Enhancing Access to Agricultural Information (EAAI) project, implemented by WOUGNET in partnership with the Technical Centre for Agriculture (CTA) and based in northern Uganda, has improved the livelihoods of women through providing relevant agricultural information to women farmers. Farmers' questions on agricultural and other topics, such as goat rearing, bean agronomy and poultry keeping, are discussed on weekly radio talk shows. Relevant agricultural information is sourced or produced, repackaged into local content and disseminated via radio and SMS as well as on audiotapes, video tapes and CD-ROMs. The content is made available in the local language, Luo.

The Radio and Internet programme (RANET) helps national and regional organisations get useful information that is locked in urban areas out to rural and remote places in the hope of promoting sustainable development and reducing disaster losses. Information on weather, water, and climate is made available to rural and remote populations in the form of environmental forecasts, observations and warnings.

Agricultural Research and Extension Network (ARENET), a web portal (http://www.meteo-uganda.net/ranet/index.htm), is dedicated to helping anyone involved in improving rural farming to readily access practical and technical agricultural information from various national and international sources. It enables service providers, rural development workers and extension agents to help the farmers in their areas by posting their questions and problems through the system to agricultural experts in the research institutes and in local government so as to solve some of their farming problems.[3]

New ICT has also been used by gender-equality advocates all over the world to disseminate rights-based information and contribute to debates on gender and rights. Actors at different levels, from multilateral agencies like UNIFEM to local feminist activists, are involved in creating, collating and disseminating material on rights – legal rights, sexual and reproductive rights, women's human rights. However, as Anita Gurumurthy points out:[4]

> the majority of women ... do not have access to new ICTs, for reasons of infrastructure, society, culture and language. While it may be necessary for the progressive elite to mediate information dissemination, real democratisation of information depends on making new ICTs relevant to the majority and accessible to every woman.

Building the capacity of women

Training in ICT can play a key role in improving the capacity of women for ICT-related jobs, and in enhancing the skills of businesswomen, entrepreneurs and professionals for career growth and improved efficiency in their work. Targeting women in situations where access to ICT is limited is important to ensure that they are equal beneficiaries of technology.

Successful projects aimed at building the skills of women include the Enhancing Income Growth among Small and Micro Women Entrepreneurs project that has empowered women who are small and micro entrepreneurs with ICT and entrepreneurship skills to manage their enterprises effectively. Women entrepreneurs are able to access relevant entrepreneurial content and disseminate success stories as well as advertise their projects through the women in the business portal (http://www.wib.or.ug). In this project women are able to access the internet using a mobile internet connection.

The WIRES project, implemented by CEEWA-Uganda, targets women entrepreneurs in small-scale businesses, addressing the need for entrepreneurial information repackaged in simple, ready-to-use formats, preferably in local languages.[5] Through the programme, women have been able to access ICT and obtain information on markets, prices, credit services and trade-support services.

Building the ICT skills of women in decision-making structures, especially government, enables them to compete effectively in a male-dominated ICT market, and to secure stable, well-paid jobs.

ICT as an amplifier of women's voices

ICT can provide spaces for diverse, bottom-up, and low-cost communication. It can amplify women's voices, and help to publicise women's experiences and perspectives, for example through using radio and video to document and disseminate information to policy makers and the public. Feminist academics and scholars have used the internet to publish perspectives that concern a range of issues.[6] This is an area that more women and women's organisations need to explore since it reflects women's perspectives and informs other women on various development issues. Documentation is also important in arguing the case in advocacy.

WOUGNET and mobile activism

In the modern era, both public and private sectors are needed to fully utilise and appreciate the effectiveness and efficiency of using mobile phones in processing, storing and retrieving information. In Uganda the government's liberalised approach to ICT has encouraged many mobile phone service providers (currently five: MTN, WARID, Zain, UTL and Orange) to extend networks to remote rural areas of Uganda. Mobile phone subscription and penetration is 8,554,864 according to December 2008 statistics by the Uganda Communications Commission. The mobile phone is the exclusive means of communication for the typical Ugandan citizen and it is gradually becoming recognised that through initiatives such as UnoPhone and the MTN Village Phone, women can provide community telephony services as a source of income.[7]

Given the broader reach of mobile phones compared to, say, the internet, the development of these community telephony services is a very welcome development. Mobile phones have advantages over the internet that include their widespread geographic coverage in terms of access, as well as the low level of skills and knowledge required to make use of them in day-to-day activities. In addition, the available mobile phone service packages facilitate access through options such as pay as you go, where a subscriber can load up the amount of airtime that they can afford, and Me2U, where one subscriber can send airtime credit to another subscriber. As a result of using mobile phones, women and women's organisations have found themselves achieving their goals in an effective way such as getting immediate responses through the use of SMS when calling members to attend meetings and workshops. The success is due to speed in manipulating information.

Since it is impossible to escape the powerful impact of mobile phones, organisations such as WOUGNET have tapped the potential of mobile phones in data collection, advocacy, networking and information sharing. According to the findings of the 2003 WOUGNET evaluation report (which used the APC Gender Evaluation Methodology (GEM) tool that is useful in assessing initiatives using ICT for social change), WOUGNET activities did increase awareness and participation among women, and did foster information sharing and networking among women and women's organisations. However, the benefits were still limited to those organisations that had access to the internet, leaving out the majority of women and women's organisations in rural areas.

Indeed, while ICT and the internet offer vast, new and unprecedented opportunities for human development and empowerment in areas ranging from education and the environment to healthcare and business, they are also one of the key contributing factors to social and economic disparities between different social and economic groups. The gender divide is one of the most significant inequalities amplified by the digital revolution and it cuts across all social and income groups. Throughout the world, women face serious challenges – economic, social and cultural – that prevent or limit their access to, use of and benefits from ICT.[8]

Over 80 per cent of Uganda's population of 29 million is rural based – the majority of whom are women. However, there are still only limited efforts made, through awareness workshops, seminars or print materials, to support women and women's organisations in the rural areas to explore ICT opportunities in their activities. Constraints for women include:

- Inadequate skills and knowledge about how to use ICT in their daily activities
- Lack of ICT centres where they could exploit ICT in their activities
- Lack of connectivity to access information disseminated online
- Lack of information translated into the local language
- Lack of diversified methods of disseminating information that would satisfy both urban and rural women
- Lack of technical skills to address problems such as computer breakdown and maintenance.

Following the 2003 evaluation, WOUGNET's overall objective was revised to strengthen the use of ICT among women and women's organisations, to build capacities in ICT use, and to expand activities to reach out to women in the rural areas. Currently, WOUGNET's activities are conducted under the guidance of the 2008–10 Strategic Plan with the overall goal of enabling women and women's organisations to use ICT strategically and innovatively for sustainable development. Among its ICT tools, WOUGNET has used mobile technology for advocacy, documentation and organisation.

In an effort to reach out to members easily and quickly, WOUGNET has made use of SMS to reach particular individuals as well as a group of members and partners. In order to facilitate communication with a group WOUGNET has, with the support of Hivos, made use of the BulkSMS tool, a web-based application that enables the distribution of SMS to a group of subscribers locally and individually. With support of Tactical Tech (see Chapter 4) and Fahamu, WOUGNET has also been able to test and apply FrontlineSMS (see Chapter 3), a package that can facilitate receiving and sending SMS via one's computer. These tools facilitate the processing and management of information.

Examples of how WOUGNET has used mobile technology for advocacy include running SMS campaigns in support of the 16 Days of Activism Against Gender Violence in 2007 and 2008 that run from 25 November to 10 December each year. On each of the 16 days, SMS were sent out on topical issues, and some of the responses to the SMS were also sent out to all the subscribers. In order to increase the outreach, as well as to integrate mobile and internet applications, all SMS sent or received during these campaigns were posted to a blog on the WOUGNET website.[9] The campaigns have drawn participants from over 20 countries in Africa, Asia, Europe, North and South America.

SMS has also been used to support women's rights-based organisations to send out awareness messages for women's day celebrations and to stand up as one voice against cases of gender-based violence. A peaceful demonstration against the escalation of cases of domestic and sexual violence against women (defilement and rape) was carried out by men and women in civil society organisations on 10 June 2008 to call on policy makers to put the plight of women on the government agenda. In this case SMS was used to mobilise people for the demonstration. The above examples show that SMS can be used strategically to promote women's rights.

WOUGNET has used SMS to support online discussions, enabling its members without email and internet access to participate in discussions. A case to note is the online discussion on how ICT can be used to create wealth. The discussion combined using mailing lists, blogging and SMS, and brought to light the role ICT can play in poverty reduction given the infrastructural and cultural environment in Uganda. Both the positive development impact and potential of ICT were exhaustively discussed. Rural participants appreciated using SMS as an initiative that would enable them to speak out on issues related to development even without internet connectivity.

The EAAI project that targets rural women farmers in northern Uganda combines mobile phones with other tools including a website, community radio and an information centre to improve the productivity of the women farmers and to enable them to access markets by providing timely and accurate information in the local language. SMS messages generated by partner organisations such as BROSDI (Busoga Rural Open Source and Development Initiative) are translated into the local language, Luo, and disseminated to women farmers.[10] Equipped and trained to use SMS, women farmers are able to contact agricultural experts for advice and to exchange information about weekly radio shows and available information materials.

A study undertaken by WOUGNET in 2008[11] confirmed the mobile phone as one of the major sources of information, next to radio. Women interviewed reported they use mobile phones to:

- Make contributions and ask for clarification during radio programmes
- Call extension workers to come and attend to their animals or advise them on a crop or method of farming
- Call their relatives for information
- Inquire about market prices for their produce
- Get learning best practices from other groups
- Get to know about the group meetings (mobilisation).

The mobile phone offers faster and cheaper communication options, often replacing long and costly journeys, as well as reducing losses through the effective use of information obtained. Information about market prices gives farmers wider options for selling their products and better prices.

Challenges

Mobile technology, especially the use of mobile phones, has helped WOUGNET achieve a number of goals in an effective way, such as calling members to attend meetings and workshops, getting immediate responses, and increasing participation of beneficiaries in projects. The success of this is due to the speed in manipulating information. However, despite these opportunities there are a number of challenges faced when implementing such technology.

A large percentage of the rural population, of which 80 per cent are women, is yet to benefit effectively from use of the mobile phone. Illiteracy is one of the limiting factors since SMS is best suited to delivering short, simple messages. This impacts on the packaging and delivery of information and services to the beneficiaries. The information has to be translated into local languages and delivered orally for the majority of the rural farmers to understand it.

Many farmers live in poverty and may not be able to afford a phone or airtime nor to pay for information services. A study by Tusubira, Kagwa and Ongora, 2005,[12] revealed that in the rural areas only about 25 per cent of the population use community telephony services fairly regularly. Regular usage in urban areas is just over 60 per cent, most likely as a result of a combination of higher income, greater ease of access and greater awareness. This makes long-term sustainability of projects difficult since they are funded by donors who expect them to be self-sustaining after a certain period.

Finding the right hardware to use is sometimes difficult. For example, as a cost-cutting strategy, the FrontlineSMS tool was designed to work with old models of phones which are cheaper. However, the data cables to link these phones to a computer are not readily available in Uganda. WOUGNET eventually solved this problem by using a GPRS wireless modem.

There is low awareness of ICT in rural areas, as compared to urban areas, and although radio and mobile are the most common ICT in the rural areas, listening to radio is constrained by time and many women still cannot afford phones.

In many rural areas, challenges to women's use of ICT still

exist due to the cultural life style that keeps females occupied in domestic work, limiting the time available for using ICT. Women still have no control over decision making nor their time, and membership of women's development groups results, in some cases, in domestic violence. A study undertaken by WOUGNET on people's information needs revealed that belonging to development groups was causing discomfort in some homes and putting pressure on women.[13] Though women are expected to look after households single-handedly, many men do not want their women to be empowered (better off). This calls for sensitisation of men to respect women's rights and for women to know their rights.

However, WOUGNET is committed to directing all its efforts to supporting women and women's organisations in Uganda to access and utilise ICT in their development activities to improve their lives.

For example, in the EAAI project SMS is used with a combination of other dissemination methods such as radio and face-to-face meetings, since most women can access only group mobile phones that have been provided with support from CTA. WOUGNET also works with partner organisations that develop agricultural content and government agricultural extension services as a way of reaching out to a wider community, avoiding duplication and ensuring the sustainability of projects. Equipping women farmers with skills on how to use ICT and develop information with local content is an approach that WOUGNET uses to cut across the problem of illiteracy, and to enable rural women farmers and other members to feel comfortable using ICT to access information. To promote local ownership of projects, WOUGNET works closely with the local government and encourages men to participate in annual community meetings; though not primarily the beneficiaries, men are allowed to participate in meetings and use the information centre.

Use of SMS for development-oriented purposes and advocacy is still limited to a few community projects and organisations. However, WOUGNET expects in the long run the rural communities, as well as urban and elite women, to realise the benefits of using SMS to improve their production and, hence, livelihoods, to network and to collaborate.

Notes

1. Tusubira, F.F., Kaggwa, I. and Ongora, J. (2005) 'Uganda', in Gillward, A. (ed), *Towards an African e-Index: Household and Individual ICT Access and Usage Across 10 African Countries* , South Africa, The Link Centre.
2. 'Bridging the rural digital divide: "e-agriculture" – a definition and profile of its application', FAO, www.fao.org/rdd, accessed 28 May 2009.
3. ARENET website, http://www.ranetproject.net, accessed 3 June 2009.
4. Gurumurthy, A. (2006) 'Promoting gender equality? Some development-related uses of ICTs by women', *Development in Practice*, vol. 16, no. 6, www.siyanda.org/docs/gurumurthy_icts.pdf, accessed 31 August 2009.
5. CEEWA website – Uganda, http://www.ceewauganda.org, accessed 3 June 2009.
6. Gurumurthy, A. (2006).
7. UCC (2008) 'Market review report December 2008: status of the communications market', http://www.ucc.co.ug , accessed 20 September 2009.
8. Palitza, K. (2007) 'Editorial', *Agenda: Feminist Media*, no. 71, http://www.agenda.org.za/content/blogcategory/2/88889071/, accessed 15 October 2009.
9. Information about the WOUGNET SMS Campaigns is online at http://www.wougnet.org/cms/index.php?option=com_content&task=blogcategory&id=63&Itemid=104.
10. BROSDI website, http://www.brosdi.or.ug, accessed 3 June 2009.
11. WOUGNET (2008) 'A baseline study on information needs, information sources, health, education, livelihoods, good governance and gender concerns of rural women in Apac District, Uganda'.
12. Tusubira et al (2005) pp. 162-77.
13. WOUGNET (2008).

9

Mobile telephony: closing the gap

Christiana Charles-Iyoha

Introduction

With about 4 billion mobile phones in use globally, the mobile phone has become the most ubiquitous communication device in the world, having experienced exponential growth, especially in countries and regions with less wired infrastructure. To an extent, its affordable, accessible and educationally appropriate access appears to facilitate digital inclusion at about all levels, therefore implying large rays of hope that the digital divide is close to being bridged and we will all soon be in 'digitopia'.

There is no doubt that mobile phones have increased teledensity in countries with less wired infrastructure. More recently, the pervasive use of mobile phones in innovative ways has opened vistas of opportunities to deep rural and peri-urban communities hitherto excluded from telecommunications services.

Globally, this new window of communications has given both voice and greater decision-making powers to disadvantaged and vulnerable groups, in addition to creating opportunities for participation in governance. This is because, through mobile phones, more people now have greater and speedier reach to information at much lower cost.

Mobile phones are increasingly becoming imposing and powerful ICT tools for participating in the global market. Mobiles have also become a key component of civil society activism and have been used successfully to mobilise large numbers of people across geographical borders in human rights campaigns. Amnesty

International has used mobile phones successfully for mobilising support for human rights campaigns. Other examples include New Tactics/SendingOutanSMS,[1] MobileActive,[2] and kiwanja. net,[3] a website that hosts a mobile applications database and is a resource on the innovative and transformative use of mobiles in development. There is also a network of civil society organisations (Pan Africa Mobile Network, PAMONET) who are actively engaged in using mobile phones for advocacy campaigns.

As emphasised in Mobiles in-a-box (see Chapter 4), advocacy using mobile phones is:

• Dynamic – unlike other communications devices, the mobile phone is usually carried with the user at all times, therefore it offers the possibility of instant, simultaneous communications.
• Diverse – the mobile phone connects previously unconnected people and new audiences through the potential viral effect of forwarding messages.
• Discreet – the camera included in many modern phones allows for filming and photography in situations where use of a conventional camera would be dangerous.
• Direct – the mobile phone allows for communication directly to and from the communities that advocates are working with.

Mobile phones provide individual users and communities with valuable access to a range of data services for personal and commercial purposes. They also allow them increased engagement in civil society and in the democratic processes of their countries. This engagement may take many forms: monitoring elections, receiving job alerts via SMS (text message), running small businesses, reporting illegal logging, accessing up-to-date market price information or providing an alternative form of media access.[4]

Mobiles have the potential to socially empower women in restrictive cultures, by aiding their interaction with men without being in the same place or having face-to-face contact, as well as to assist women in organising and coordinating campaigns and advocacy targeted at fostering women's inclusion in good governance.

Innovative applications of mobile phones in education, health and even financial transactions provide women with economic empowerment, increased learning opportunities, and improved market access for their products as they easily access more timely information, more services and, to an extent, gain more voice in public affairs as they can send text messages on issues of public policy concern.

Besides, there is growing consensus amongst development workers and even technologists that mobile phones can play an important role in reducing poverty, improving education and healthcare, enhancing political participation and empowerment, as well as facilitating the achievement of some of the millennium development goals, thereby promoting sustainable development.

This role of mobile phones as tools for development and socio-economic transformation, coupled with the opportunities mobile activism presents for more effective civil society campaigns and advocacy that facilitates inclusion at all levels, is huge. However, the opportunities for the use of this technology for advocacy and inclusion are undermined by poverty, culture and urban bias in connectivity.

Poverty

The high poverty levels in Africa impact women significantly more than men, thereby accounting for the critical disparities between men and women in access to mobile phones and the range of services offered. The buying power of economically disadvantaged women is very limited – to food and very basic essentials – which denies this group of women access to exclusive ownership of this communication device. Financial poverty therefore excludes poor women from the emerging benefits of the many innovative uses of mobile phones.

Women, as a group, account for over 70 per cent of people living in poverty, particularly in developing and least-developed economies, and 50 per cent of the populace worldwide generally. In Africa, women form nearly 50 per cent of a population that is under very heavy pressures from a social organisational pattern that is inherently unprepared for the actualisation of the millennium development goals, sustainable development and the socio-economic transformation of poor, vulnerable and marginalised peoples, largely located in the rural and peri-urban areas.

Women's poverty is further heightened by limited or no access to productive resources. The Food and Agriculture Organisation (FAO) recently noted that the contribution of women and girls would be far greater if they were able to have equal access to essential resources and services. They also found that women in rural areas were even more disadvantaged, with far less access to information and technology than men. This naturally limited both their influence and their ability to participate in decision-making processes.[5]

The unequal power relations between men and women contribute to differential access to the effective use of mobile phones for participation and involvement in the several innovative ways this technology is being used to foster inclusion in nearly every aspect of life.

Culture

In restrictive cultures, certain socio-cultural and religious norms that prohibit women from using public access points also limit the potential of mobile phones to have an impact on entire populations. Apart from the fact that many poor women who cannot afford to own a mobile phone are excluded from the mainstream of this communication device's usage and influence, their limited status in the home also affects their ability to use their husband's phone as even such usage is very likely to be restricted to taking place only when the husband is at home with the wife. Additionally, patriarchal, culturally defined roles that locate women in time-consuming activities in the care economy can limit women's optimisation of this technology for participation and inclusion.

Urban bias in connectivity

Though Africa is currently experiencing exponential growth in ownership and use of mobile phones, the fact remains that a number of rural communities are still largely excluded from accessing this telecommunication service on account of both the cost of acccess and a lack of network coverage. However, this is a temporary setback as mobile phone service providers are working hard to ensure mobile network coverage in deep rural communities.

Expertise

The knowledgeable and effective use of mobile phones amongst urban, peri-urban and rural women can expand their access to knowledge, economic opportunities and centres of decision-making, as well as facilitate their participation and inclusion in decision-making at all levels of society.

Additionally, capacitating women in this way could facilitate the achievement of the millennium development goals in Africa as women using mobile phones for next generation services would more easily find spaces to organise and connect across geographical boundaries. For example, the results of a study on mobile phone usage for agricultural information mining in south-western Uganda indicates that more male farmers (59.3 per cent) used phones than female farmers (40.7 per cent). However, more female (66.7 per cent) than male farmers (33.3 per cent) requested information on natural resource management (NRM) and agriculture.[6]

The analysis of gender in the use of the phones across the parishes found that more male farmers made use of the phones in two parishes (Rwanyana – 77.9 per cent and Mugandu – 60 per cent) while more female farmers (66.7 per cent) made use of the telephone in Kitooma parish. The analysis of the purpose of phone calls showed that women used the phone to request information on NRM and agriculture more than men across the three parishes, while men used the phone more for personal calls and to look for market information.

In conclusion, mobile phones present opportunities for focusing efforts on increasing women's participation, empowerment and transformation through inclusion in the decision-making process in an effective and powerful way. This would both bridge the gender digital divide and achieve competitive and fair inclusion at all levels. Such participation would also ensure that gender issues were taken into account in development policy.

Recommendations

An urgent, but very strategic, inclusive and cascadable programme of engagement activities with women's organisations across Africa is proposed. Such a programme will use the machinery of women's networks in Africa, grassroots women's organisations, the media, parliamentarians, policy makers, ICT institutions and the private sector to develop a community of rural women as mobile telephony socio-economic resource experts engaged in building rural knowledge economies to fast track the inclusion and knowledgeable participation of African rural women in the global knowledge economy.

The project will strengthen rural women's capacity to use mobile phones by setting up basic pay-phone call centres that provide some protection from the elements. These will enable women to use mobile phones not only to make and receive calls but also to access next-generation services and, ultimately, to network, collaborate, access pertinent development information and even work on advocacy. The self-sustaining mobile telephony-mediated access and capacity-building point, comprising a mobile phone call centre, will serve as a mediated access point to facilitate the participation and inclusion of a large number of women in peri-urban and rural areas in the growing annual international 16 Days of Activism Against Gender Violence and other such gender-related programmes. In 2007, WOUGNET[7] (see Chapter 8), in collaboration with Womensnet, South Africa and APC Africa Women (AAW), conducted an SMS-based campaign, sending out SMS on each of the 16 Days of Activism that would encourage individuals and organisations to speak out, stand out, and commit to preventing violence against women. There were over 170 participants drawn from 13 countries in Africa, Asia, Europe, North and South America. Individuals could contribute a short message or slogan on the theme of the campaign. The chosen slogan was sent out via SMS with the individual/organisation credited as the source of the message. People could also send news of the activities and events they organised in support of the 16 Days of Activism. Individuals could also register their mobile number to receive the SMS that were sent out during the 16 Days of Activism. The daily SMS were posted to a blog on the Take Back the Tech campaign website[8] and the WOUGNET blog.[9]

The mobile phone call centre will also provide a help line for medical and social emergencies and a capacity-building centre where disadvantaged women who have never seen or touched a phone will learn about the technology and its numerous benefits. Such a centre would facilitate a forum for the interaction of women and girls in addition to creating space for disadvantaged women to embrace the present and emerging benefits of mobile phones by offering an ICT that is accessible, affordable and appropriate to their literacy levels. Such a centre may just be all that economically and educationally vulnerable women located either in urban or rural areas need in order to organise, adopt and adapt to the information society as well as to participate in mobile-enabled social actions that advocate women's issues.

Gendered capacitating projects should address the livelihood challenges of rural and peri-urban women's current limited access to knowledge, resources, economic opportunities for sustainable livelihoods and access to centres of decision-making, alongside the need for proficient use and ownership of mobile phones. The programme would therefore, through interactive information services enabled by an enhanced capacity to use mobile phones for information management, facilitate access to development information on agriculture and health, to financial and basic social services, and to information on government support services.

The dissemination of life-transforming development information through mobile phones, as well as capacity building on optimal mobile phone usage to bottom-of-the-pyramid individuals in rural and peri-urban communities in Africa, will hopefully facilitate the full participation of women in Africa's emerging knowledge economy as well as the global knowledge economy.

A pilot study in Lesotho indicates that access to mobile phones has transformed the lives of rural women farmers, boosting income and expanding knowledge.

> The phone has transformed the women farmers' lives completely – they are able to market their produce, access information on prices, and it has made them so confident.[10]

This programme will broaden the pathways to inclusion and good governance through the use of a technology that is readily accessible, affordable and available even in remote communities where the literacy challenge hitherto impeded the use of computers and computer-based internet for information flows.

Notes

1. New Tactics, http://www.newtactics.org, accessed 21 June 2009.

2. MobileActive, www.mobileactive.org, accessed 21 June 2009.

3. kiwanja.net, www.kiwanja.net, accessed 21 June 2009.

4. Tactical Tech, Mobiles in-a-box, http//mobiles.tacticaltech.org, accessed 21 June 2009.

5. FAO – Various articles, http://tinyurl.com/n6fpwl, accessed 21 June 2009.

6. Masuki, K.F.G., Mowo, J.G., Tanui, J., Tukahirwa, J., Kamugisha, R., Ayesiga, R. and Adera E.O. (2008) 'Mobile applications in improving communication and information delivery for agricultural development in Uganda: Challenges and opportunities', paper presented at the 1st Workshop on Mobile Application for Development (M4D) in East Africa, Kampala, November.

7. WOUGNET, www.wougnet.org, accessed 21 June 2009.

8. Take Back The Tech, http://www.takebackthetech.net/blogathon, accessed 21 June 2009.

9. WOUGNET blog, http://www.wougnet.org/cms/index.php?option=com_mamblog&Itemid=83, accessed 21 June 2009.

10. *IRIN News, Lesotho* (2009) 'Women farmers get mobile phone know-how', 4 June, accessed 17 June 2009.

10

Digitally networked technology in Kenya's 2007–08 post-election crisis

Joshua Goldstein and Juliana Rotich

Introduction

On 1 January 2008, as word spread throughout Kenya that incumbent presidential candidate Mwai Kibaki had rigged the recent presidential election, text messages urging violence spread across the country, and tribal and politically-motivated attacks were perpetrated throughout Kenya.

By 9 January, as the violence escalated out of control in the Kibera slums in Nairobi and the towns of Kisumu, Kakamega, Eldoret, and Naivasha in the Rift Valley, a group of Kenyans in Nairobi and the diaspora launched Ushahidi, an online campaign to draw local and global attention to the violence taking place in their country. Within weeks, they had documented, in detail, hundreds of incidents of violence that would have otherwise gone unreported, and received hundreds of thousands of site visits from around the world, sparking increased global media attention.

Both of these anecdotes illustrate what Yochai Benkler calls the 'networked public sphere', the notion that our information environment is characterised by both the potential for many-to-many communications (instead of just one-to-one or one-to-many), and the near elimination of the cost of communication.[1] These anecdotes also represent opposite impulses on a continuum described by political scientist Larry Diamond.[2] On one side of this continuum is the 'predatory society', where behaviour is driven by cynical, opportunistic and often violent norms. On the other side, there is the 'civil society', where behaviour is driven by the norms of toleration, accountability and equality.

This chapter is largely descriptive, but also has a normative element. First, as an early cut at history, it attempts to describe the way technology was used in the aftermath of the Kenyan election. Specifically, this chapter describes three important ways that Kenyans used new technology to coordinate action: SMS campaigns to promote violence, blogs to challenge mainstream media narratives, and online campaigns to promote awareness of human rights violations.

Africa's fragile democracies

There has been some growth in the number of democracies in Africa, but the struggle between dictatorship and democracy is far from settled in much of the continent. Dictatorship looms large in obvious places like Zimbabwe, where Robert Mugabe has ignored elections and caused hyperinflation of over one million per cent per year, but also in less obvious places like Uganda, where Yoweri Museveni has extended the constitution to allow himself to run for a third term.

Even in the very countries where the predatory impulse is gaining ground, the civic impulse has seen progress. In Zimbabwe, for example, SW Radio Africa, which bills itself as the 'Independent Voice of Zimbabwe', has actively challenged the Mugabe regime. In Uganda, Andrew Mwenda, a prominent journalist, has launched the *Independent*,[3] a newspaper that provides an alternative to media outlets held closely by the government.

In Africa's struggle between democracy and dictatorship, does digital technology matter? The short answer is that there is not enough data to answer this question. Mobile phones and the internet have simply not been around long enough in Africa. It bears consideration that digital technology adoption is on the rise, and digital tools are being used in advocacy. Incidents like the crisis in Kenya provide a flash of insight into the emerging power of these tools. Additionally, theorists such as Yochai Benkler provide useful language to help us begin to understand the place of these tools in society. Benkler's notion of the networked public sphere describes two ways that digital technology enables different kinds of communication from their analogue antecedents. Benkler writes:

> The first element is the shift from a hub-and-spoke architecture with unidirectional links to the end points in the mass media, to distributed architecture with multidirectional connections among all nodes in the networked information environment. The second is the practical elimination of communications costs as a barrier to speaking across associational boundaries.[4]

In other words, digital technology offers tools that, in addition to allowing communication in the traditional one-to-one fashion, also allow us to become our own broadcasters, and reach large numbers of people in unprecedented ways at trivial cost. Viewed through the lens of this theoretical framework, the remainder of this chapter is an attempt to understand how digital technology played a role in a moment where the predatory and the civic impulses of Kenya collided violently.

Mirrors of violence

As Kenyans waited for the results of the 27 December 2007 presidential election, observers noticed Orange Democratic Movement (ODM) candidate Raila Odinga's lead of over one million votes strangely morph into a small margin of victory for the incumbent Mwai Kibaki.[5] Suspicions and tensions grew until 30 December, when the Election Commission declared Kibaki the winner at the Kenyatta International Conference Centre. Following the announcement, the Ministry of Security ordered the suspension of all live broadcasts, and the country erupted into violence. Clashes between protestors and police were worst in the Kibera slums of Nairobi, and in the ODM-dominated towns of Kisumu and later Naivasha in the Rift Valley. The violence following the election left 1,000 dead and 500,000 displaced.[6]

To a significant extent, the post-election riots were the latest embodiment of long-standing grievances of those in Kenya's Rift Valley. Following Kenya's independence from Great Britain, much of the best land went to Kenyatta's Kikuyu ethnic group, instead of the groups to whom it belonged before the British arrived.[7]

This continued under Daniel Arap Moi, who designed 'settlement schemes' that distributed land to connected political elites instead of those with historical ties to the land. Particularly since the 1991 reinstatement of multi-party politics in Kenya, the Rift Valley has faced repeated violence with each election cycle. University of Oxford scholar David Anderson estimates that, 'according to satellite mapping of the violence in the Rift Valley, 95 per cent of the recent clashes in that area have occurred on land affected by these [settlement] schemes'.[8]

Much of the violence in this region is motivated by 'majimboism', which comes from a Kiswahili term referring to the aspiration of a type of federalism composed of semi-independent regions organised by ethnic group. To many in the Rift Valley, however, majimboism legitimises violence against Kikuyus, who are seen as encroaching on the ancestral land of other ethnic groups.[9]

Viral hatred

Unavailable during earlier upheavals, mobile phones made hateful and violent messages easier and cheaper to transmit during the latest surge of violence. On 1 January 2008, Kenyans started to receive frightening text messages that urged readers to express their frustrations with the election outcome by attacking other ethnic groups. One such message reads, 'Fellow Kenyans, the Kikuyus have stolen our children's future ... we must deal with them in a way they understand ... violence.' In reaction, another reads 'No more innocent Kikuyu blood will be shed. We will slaughter them right here in the capital city. For justice, compile a list of Luos you know ... we will give you numbers to text this information.'[10]

Mass SMS tools are remarkably useful for organising this type of explicit, systematic and publicly organised campaign of mob violence. Human Rights Watch quotes a community organiser in Kalenjin as saying, 'if there is any sign that Kibaki is wining, they war should break ...They said the first step is to burn the Kikuyu homes in the village, then we will go to Turbo town, [and] after finishing Turbo they we organise to go to Eldoret ... They were coaching the young people how to go on to war [sic].'[11]

These messages are part of a troubling trend in East Africa. In April 2007, three Ugandans died in Kampala when violent acts were organised via SMS to protest against the government of Uganda's sale of the Mabira Forest to Kakira Sugar Works.[12]

While further investigation into this subject is needed, it is worth noting that there are signs that those who attempted to seek majimboism through targeted violence achieved their goals to a large extent. Human Rights Watch reports that:

> The events of the first months of 2008 have dramatically altered the ethnic makeup of many parts of Kenya. Scores of communities across the Rift Valley, including most of Eldoret itself, are no longer home to any Kikuyu residents. The rural areas outside of Naivasha, Nakuru, and Molo are similarly emptying of Kikuyu while Kalenjin and Luo are leaving the urban areas. In Central Province, few non-Kikuyu remain. The slums of Mathare, Kibera and others in Nairobi have been carved into enclaves where vigilantes from one ethnic group or another patrol 'their' areas.[13]

However, since SMS, unlike radio, is a multi-directional tool, there is also hope that voices of moderation can make themselves heard. In 1994 in Rwanda radio was used to mobilise the genocide, and moderate voices were unable to respond.[14] In Kenya, as hateful messages extended their reach into the Kenyan population, Michael Joseph, the CEO of Safaricom, Kenya's largest mobile phone provider, was approached by a government official who was considering shutting down the SMS system. Joseph convinced the government not to shut it down, but instead to allow SMS providers to send out messages of peace and calm, which Safaricom did to all nine million of its customers.

Further, it is quite easy for governments and companies to identify and track individuals who promote hate speech. In the aftermath of the violence, contact information for over 1,700 individuals who allegedly promoted mob violence was forwarded to the government of Kenya.[15] While Kenya does not yet have an applicable law to prosecute SMS-based hate speech, a debate has already begun in parliament to create such a law.[16]

In Kenya, as in the rest of Africa, SMS is the most widely used digital application. Yet a similar tension between predatory and civic speech existed on online bulletin boards. The leading Kenyan online community, Mashada,[17] became overwhelmed with divisive and hostile messages. By the end of January 2008, the moderators decided to shut down the site, recognising that civil discourse was rapidly becoming impossible. However, a few days later, Mashada's site administrator David Kobia launched I Have No Tribe,[18] a site explicitly centred on constructive dialogue amongst Kenyans. As Harvard scholar Ethan Zuckerman writes:

> [I Have No Tribe] showed posts from Kenyans around the country and around the world wrestling with the statement, 'I have no tribe … I am Kenyan'. Kobia redirected the Mashada site to the new site, and it rapidly filled with comments, combative as well as supportive, as well poems and prayers. Kobia reopened [Mashada] on 14 February having elegantly demonstrated that one possible response to destructive speech online is to encourage constructive speech.

The examples of SMS and online bulletin boards illustrate the tension inherent in new many-to-many digital communications tools. In the Kenyan context, this architecture is a new space where the predatory impulse to deepen existing cultural divides meets head on the civic impulse for constructive and healing dialogue.

Crowdsourcing human rights

Within a week of the outbreak of violence in Kenya, a small group of concerned Kenyans, located throughout the diaspora, came together to launch an online campaign called Ushahidi to spread awareness about the violence devastating their country.

Ushahidi is part of a tradition of Kenyan digital civic projects dating back at least to 2006, when Kenyan lawyer Ory Okolloh teamed up with an anonymous blogger known as 'M' to create Mzalendo: Eye on Kenyan Parliament,[19] a website dedicated to helping hold Kenyan members of parliament (MPs) accountable for their votes.

In the tradition of Mzalendo, several groups of concerned Kenyans, both in-country and in the diaspora, gathered in the immediate aftermath of the Kenyan election to launch civic initiatives. These initiatives included fundraising campaigns such as the

'Help Kenyans in Distress' campaign, which leveraged SMS money-transfer technology to support the Red Cross. Another notable example is the blog of Joseph Karoki,[20] who wrote about a little boy left crying after his mother was killed in Naivasha. He organised donations for 'baby Brian', and kept readers of his blog updated on the progress of one family affected by the violence in Kenya.

Far and away the most prominent and successful digital civic campaign was Ushahidi.[21] On 3 January, Ory Okolloh provided the spark for the project:

> Google Earth supposedly shows in great detail where the damage is being done on the ground. It occurs to me that it will be useful to keep a record of this, if one is thinking long-term. For the reconciliation process to occur at the local level the truth of what happened will first have to come out. Guys looking to do something – [are there] any techies out there willing to do a mashup of where the violence and destruction is occurring using Google maps?[22]

David Kobia and Erik Hersman, two technologists with roots in Kenya, answered the call. Leading a small group of designers, they designed and launched Ushahidi on 9 January. Ushahidi is a mashup: a blending of two internet applications to relay information in a visually compelling way. The design teams combined Google maps, which allows users to zoom in and view satellite images of Kenya, with a tool for users, via mobile phone or internet browser, to report incidents of violence on the map, add photos, video and written content that document where and when violence occurs.

In the tradition of using Google maps for human rights awareness, Ushahidi follows the Darfur Museum Mapping Initiative, a collaboration of Google Earth and the US Holocaust Museum, launched in early 2007. This platform allows the user to view professionally collected photos, video and written testimony from Darfur, as well as view images of destroyed villages and camps for internally displaced people or IDPs.

An interactive map is a remarkably effective narrative tool for a transnational audience. Tragic violence calls for empathy and action, but it is difficult to feel a connection with a place one cannot imagine. C.J. Minard's famous map of Napoleon's march to

Moscow[23] is often hailed as the best statistical graphic ever made, because it is an emotive visual presentation of the decimation of nearly half a million troops in the frigid Russian winter of 1812. Mashups like Ushahidi do not share Minard's aspiration for statistical accuracy, but they do share his desire to demonstrate to the audience the real human meaning behind numbers.

However, Ushahidi is fundamentally different from the Darfur initiative in an important way. The Ushahidi platform is revolutionary for human rights campaigns in the way that Wikipedia is revolutionary for encyclopaedias: they are tools that allow cooperation on a massive scale. Yochai Benkler describes this phenomenon as 'commons-based peer production', and argues that it has a central place in rethinking economic and social cooperation in a digital age. He writes:

> What makes peer-production enterprises work best has been the capacity to harness many people, with many and diverse motivations, towards common goals in concerted effort. While understudied and difficult to predict and manage by comparison to a more simple picture of human motivation as driven by personal wealth maximisation, peer production begins to offer a rich texture in which to study the much more varied and multifarious nature of human motivation and effective human action.[24]

In the Kenyan context, reporting an act of violence was perhaps the only outlet for frustrated citizens. As Kenyan blogger, Daudi Were, writes, 'We as Kenyans are guilty of having short-term memories. Yesterday's villains are today's heroes. We sweep bad news and difficult decision[s] under the carpet; we do not confront the issues in our society, and get shocked when the country erupts as it did two months ago.'[25]

Echoing this sentiment, Hersman writes, 'Sometimes there is just nothing more you can do than report what you see'.[26] In 2008 Hersman and Kobia launched a new version of the Ushahidi platform for use by activists interested in large-scale participation in civic campaigns. The platform is rapidly making an impact in the humanitarian relief community. For example, Patrick Meier, a PhD candidate at the Fletcher School of Law and Diplomacy at Tufts University, is applying the lessons of Ushahidi to humanitarian early warning systems.

Meier is developing a tool called the Humanitarian Sensor Web,[27] which allows community leaders and service providers like the World Food Programme to coordinate their efforts in emergency humanitarian situations. Further, the Sensor Web aims to serve as a source of collective intelligence, with a map-based database of places and events, which will help those who are responding to current crises or planning for future security or humanitarian relief.

While these tools are still in an experimental stage, Ushahidi has significantly lowered the costs of participating in a global civic campaign from anywhere on the planet with wireless network coverage. This is achieved by integrating FrontlineSMS (see Chapter 3 and Figure 10.1[28]) with Ushahidi to enable SMS sync with the web. An SMS hub can then be created and run by a local administrator, who can filter the messages and add more detail before publishing the reports onto the mapping.

This capability is very important for areas that do not have internet access; their voices can still be heard through the use of mobile phones. The Ushahidi platform is currently working on an alert system to which users can sign up to receive either an email or SMS when an incident is reported in a specified area. This has the potential to further democratise society by encouraging participation by anyone with a mobile phone. An Ushahidi instance can act as a node for the SMS network, with a bridge to the cloud that is the web.

Citizen voices

Just as human rights activists used digital tools to amplify their voice and lower their cost of operations, so too did citizen journalists, who used blogs to challenge the narrative presented by mainstream Kenyan media and the government.[29] The notion that citizen journalists are changing the media landscape in rich countries with ubiquitous internet access is now well understood. However, the power and influence of bloggers is particularly noteworthy in Kenya, where less than five per cent of Kenyans have regular internet access.[30] Kenyan bloggers became a critical part of the national conversation, starting during the three-day ban on live broadcasts, when the web traffic from within Kenya shot through the roof.

Figure 10.1 SMS reporting through Ushahidi[28]

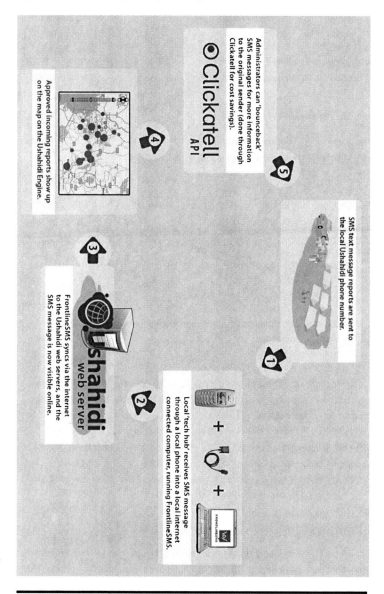

It is important to note that Kenya has perhaps the richest blogging tradition in sub-Saharan Africa. The first Kenyan blogger, Daudi Were, launched his personal blog, Mentalacrobatics, in March 2003.[31] Starting in 2004, the community began to grow rapidly among digitally connected Kenyans, who self-organised into blog rings that serve as online directories. Most prominently, the Kenyan Blogs Webring[32] currently tracks 800 blogs with a popular aggregator called KenyaUnlimited, which is administered by Were. It is not a coincidence that Were was part of the team verifying reports for the Ushahidi project. Bloggers were the early supporters of Ushahidi and they are the ones who spread word of the SMS number to Kenyans with no internet access.

When the Government of Kenya declared a ban on live news coverage on 30 December 2007, Kenyan bloggers became indispensable in their role as citizen journalists. As press critic Jay Rosen writes, citizen journalists are:

> the people formerly known as the audience [who] were on the receiving end of a media system that ran one way, in a broadcasting pattern, with high entry fees and a few firms competing to speak very loudly while the rest of the population listened in isolation from one another – and who today are not in a situation like that at all ... The people formerly known as the audience are simply the public made realer, less fictional, more able, less predictable.[33]

During the post-election crisis period, blogs became a critical source of information for Kenyans in Nairobi and the diaspora. Rumours spread via SMS were dispelled via online dialogue that took place on blogs and in the comments section of blogs.[34] All digital tools came into play at this time and aggregation of all this content became useful in filtering the torrent of information coming in various forms. This is what drove the creation of a crowd-sourcing platform like Ushahidi.

Conclusion

To all but the most entrenched old guard in the developed world, the term 'networked public sphere' connotes a more plentiful public discourse, increased transparency and positive cooperation of all kinds. Throughout sub-Saharan Africa, where artificial borders and legacies of ethnic strife have yet to solidify many countries into nations, the narrative is more complicated. This chapter has shown that, in the Kenyan context, whether aspiring to promote an ethnic-based hate crime or a global human rights campaign, the internet and mobile phones have lowered the barriers to participation and increased opportunities for many-to-many communication. Clay Shirky gets to the heart of the matter: 'The current change, in one sentence, is this: most of the barriers to group action have collapsed, and without those barriers, we are free to explore new ways of gathering together and getting things done'.[35] As the ubiquity of digital communication increases in Africa, we will no doubt see the struggle between predatory violence and civil society continue. Additionally, with increasing use of mobile phones, platforms for enabling civic engagement and advocacy through SMS will grow in importance. Tools like Ushahidi will be useful not only in advocacy via mobile phones, but also in showcasing the information online to a wider audience.

A longer version of this case study is part of a series produced by the Internet and Democracy Project, a research initiative at the Berkman Center for Internet & Society that investigates the impact of the internet on civic engagement and democratic processes. More information on the Internet and Democracy Project can be found at http://cyber.law. harvard.edu/research/internetdemocracy.

Notes

1. Benkler, Y. (2006) *Wealth of Networks: How Social Production Transforms Markets and Freedom*, New Haven, Yale University Press.
2. Diamond, L. (2001) 'Civic communities and predatory societies', delivered at Culture Matters: A Forum on Business, Education, and Training Professionals, Washington DC, http://stanford.edu/~ldiamond/papers/ civicPredatory.pdf, accessed 16 September 2009.
3. *The Independent – Uganda*, http://www.independent.co.ug/.
4. Benkler, Y. (2006) p. 212.
5. Kenyans for Peace with Truth and Justice (2008) 'Countdown to deception: 30 hours that destroyed Kenya', *Kenya National Commission on Human Rights*, 17 January, http://www.knchr.org/dmdocuments/KPTJ_Final_Press_Release. pdf, accessed 19 September 2009.
6. Human Rights Watch (2008) 'Ballots to bullets: organised political violence and Kenya's crisis of government', http://hrw.org/reports/2008/kenya0308/

kenya0308web.pdf, accessed 2 June 2009.
7. Kenya National Commission on Human Rights (2006) *Unjust Enrichment: The Making of Land Grabbing Millionaires*, p. 1.
8. Human Rights Watch (2008), p. 13.
9. See, for example, Anderson, D. (2008) 'Majimboism: the troubled history of an idea', in Branch D. and Cheeseman N. (eds) *Our Turn to Eat! Politics in Kenya since 1950*, Berlin, Lit Verlag.
10. Quist-Arcton, O. 'Text messages used to incite violence in Kenya', *NPR News*, http://www.npr.org/templates/story/story.php?storyId=19188853.
11. Human Rights Watch (2008) p. 37.
12. See, for example, http://inanafricanminute.blogspot.com/2007/04/dark-side-of-mobilisation.html, accessed 2 June 2009.
13. Ibid. p. 56.
14. 'Make text not war', Humanitarian.info, http://www.humanitarian.info/2008/04/24/make-text-not-war/
15. Querengesser, T. (2008) 'Hate speech SMS offenders already tracked', *The Nation*, 1 March, http://allafrica.com/stories/200802291070.html, accessed 2 June 2009.
16. Wanjiku, R. (2006) 'Kenya moves to thwart mobile phone crimes', *The Standard*, 16 May, http://www.thestandard.com/news/2008/05/16/kenya-moves-thwart-mobile-phone-crimes, accessed 2 June 2009.
17. WhiteAfrican.com, 'Mashada forums: Kenya's first digital casualty' http://whiteafrican.com/2008/01/29/mashada-forums-kenyas-first-digital-casualty/.
18. 'I have no tribe', http://ihavenotribe.com/.
19. Mzalendo: eye on Parliament, http://www.mzalendo.com/about/, accessed 19 September 2009.
20. Joseph Karoki blog, 'Found alive and well', http://josephkaroki.wordpress.com/2008/02/11/found-alive-and-well/.
21. Ushahidi, 'Crowdsourcing crisis information', http://legacy.ushahidi.com/about.asp.
22. Kenya Pundit, 'Update 3 January 11.00 pm', http://www.kenyanpundit.com/2008/01/03/update-jan-3-445-1100-pm/.
23. C.J. Minard's Map of Napoleon's March of 1812, Donoho Design Group, http://www.ddg.com/LIS/InfoDesignF96/Kelvin/Napoleon/map.html.
24. Benkler, Y. and Nissenbaum, H. (2006) 'Commons-based peer production and virtue', *The Journal of Political Philosophy*, vol. 14, no. 4, p. 403, accessed 19 September 2009.
25. Mentalacrobatics, http://www.mentalacrobatics.com/think/.
26. White African, 'Mapping Zimbabwe's election breaches', http://whiteafrican.com/?p=957.
27. 'Crisis mapping and early warning', http://hhi.harvard.edu/programs-and-research/crisis-mapping-and-early-warning.
28. http://blog.ushahidi.com/index.php/2008/11/05/sms-reporting-through-ushahidi/.
29. This section explicitly addresses how the blogosphere affected the narrative within Kenya. Others are extensively studying how news source

from the developing world are shaping developed world narratives. See, for example, Zuckerman, E. (2003) 'Global attention profiles – a working paper – first steps towards a quantitative approach to the study of media attention', Harvard's Berkman Center for Internet and Society Working Paper Series, http://cyber.law.harvard.edu/publications/2003/Global_Attention_Profiles.

30. Internet penetration is notoriously difficult to measure in Africa, where the majority of internet users have shared access, primarily through internet cafes. While publicly available figures put access at 1.5 per cent, this only refers to broadband subscriptions, which account for a tiny percentage of access.

31. Mentalacrobatics, 'Ferocious in battle, magnanimous in victory', http://www.mentalacrobatics.com/think/archives/2003/03, accessed 2 June 2009.

32.Kenya Unlimited, 'Kenya Blogs Webring', http://www.kenyaunlimited.com/kenyan-blogs-webring/, accessed 2 June 2009.

33. Rosen, J. (2007) 'The People Formerly Known as the Audience', *PressThink*, 17 September, http://journalism.nyu.edu/pubzone/weblogs/pressthink/2006/06/27/ppl_frmr.html#more, accessed 9 August 2007.

34. Mentalacrobatics, 'ODM Press Conference – Kenya Election 2007', http://www.mentalacrobatics.com/think/archives/2007/12/odm_press_conference_kenya_election_2007.php, accessed 2 June 2009.

35. Shirky, C. (2008) *Here Comes Everybody: The Power of Organizing Without Organizations*, New York, Penguin, p. 22.

11

Using mobile phones for monitoring human rights violations in the DRC

Bukeni Waruzi

The mobile phone is, today, among the most pervasive and signif-icant of communication technologies in the Democratic Republic of Congo (DRC). The impact of mobile phones has been felt in all regions of the country, across all generations and all aspects of social and economic life. Although our comparative study focussed on the eastern part of the country, we can confidently say that the findings apply to other regions as well. Despite the fact that mobile phones remain a subject of controversy with regard to mining companies exploiting the country's resources, notably coltan, they remain an indispensable tool, especially in a country where communication would otherwise be impossible. The little landline infrastructure that exists dates back to the colonial era.

The use of mobile phones differs from rural to urban areas, with a different set of values linked to either milieu. There has been an attempt to achieve a balance between the two, based on similar needs, demand and use. Mobile telephony has become a major phenomenon and is central to socio-economic activity: money transfers, communication and access to information. The mobile telephony market in Africa has grown twice as fast as the global market and has, at the same time, provided greater access to opportunities for the continent's population. Mobile telephony accounts for 90 per cent of new telephone subscriptions. This is true for the DRC as elsewhere. In spite of all of this, communica-tion technology remains underdeveloped in DRC.

There is an increasing number of mobile telephone operators in the country, notably Vodacom, CELTEL, CCT (Congo Chine

Telecom) and Tigo. The presence of these network operators has ensured significant national coverage. Although prices vary from one operator to the next, there is virtually total national coverage, save for a few isolated areas that are still unreachable. This has allowed for the use of mobile phones for various socio-economic activities.

This chapter presents an overview of the use of mobile phones in human rights work, namely monitoring and reporting of abuses of children's rights.

In 2005, the United Nations Security Council adopted Resolution 1612, which deals with monitoring and reporting on violations of the rights of children in situations of armed conflict, notably in Burundi, DRC, Chad, Sudan, Sri Lanka, Myanmar and Uganda.

The resolution set out to establish a mechanism for collecting data on violations of the rights of children in armed conflict. But data collection in a country like DRC can only be carried out using strategies that take into account the existing challenges.

Human rights organisations, especially those concerned with children's rights, use the mobile phone as a tool for collecting and reporting information and data on children's rights abuses. The Youth for Integrated Development – Kalundu Child Soldier project (AJEDI-Ka/PES) used a number of significant mechanisms for data collection on violations of children's rights. AJEDI-Ka/ PES is a local organisation that works to demobilise, reintegrate and rehabilitate child soldiers and other young people affected by armed conflicts in the Uvira region of South Kivu Province, to the east of the country. The organisation works within local communities in supporting child survivors of violence committed by armed militias.

The organisation chose to use mobile phones to collect data on violations of children's rights. To this end, the organisation set up 14 village committees for the protection of children's rights (CVPE) in up to 25 villages in the Uvira region (in the Uvira and Fizi areas), each seen to be high-risk areas for young people. Each CVPE has five members, generally including a teacher, an elder in the community, a member of the local church, a member of the local administration and a business leader, each representing a particular religious, social or economic category in the village, as well as, in some instances, former child soldiers.[1] Some of the members have received training in use of mobile phones for reporting children's rights violations.

The role of the members is to collect information on rights violations in their village and send these by mobile phone to the AJEDI office located in central Uvira, which then notifies the relevant authorities for eventual action. We call this the 'collection-reportage-response' mechanism. The reports are quite detailed and include the age and sex of the child, what they were doing at the time they were violated, the nature of the violation and injuries received, length of violation and what the victim and witnesses would like to see happen to the perpetrators.[2]

According to the organisation's records, a total of 135 violations were reported in 2007 – an average of 11 cases per month. The most recurrent violations were sexual abuse of minors between the ages of 9 and 13 years, torture, rape and forced or underage marriage. The main perpetrators were the armed groups operating in the area – government troops, the Mai-Mai militia, the local police – as well as civilians.

This information is collected from villages in the eastern part of DRC and then sent to the organisation's principal partner, the Watchlist on Children and Armed Conflicts, who in turn process it before forwarding it to the UN Security Council. Some of this information is included in the secretary-general's report on children and armed conflict (together with material from other UN agencies). Children's rights fall under the ambit of the under-secretary-general and special envoy for children and armed conflicts. Analysis of the number of recorded violations showed a marked drop between 2007 and early 2009. In February 2009 the organisation recorded 8 violations in 14 villages, using about 3,550 mobile call units.

The high incidence of violations has led to the development of various victim-assistance strategies. These strategies have been employed in safeguarding rights to information on contraceptives and also, in the case of Ushahidi[3] (see Chapter 10), reporting human rights violations by means of a 24-hour, free hotline. These strategies have had some positive results. For example the hotline set up by Population Service International (PSI) and Association Santé Familiale (ASF) provided valuable contraception information to women, leading to a drop in pregnancy rates from 15 per cent to 6 per cent. A special agreement was signed with Vodacom, and the number of calls recorded in the Kinshasa region from 2003 to 2008 was between 600 and 2,000.

Another excellent example was the decision at the end of 2008, to use the Ushahidi platform[4] to set up a hotline for reporting outbreaks of violence in North Kivu, during the skirmishes between government troops and the rebels under Laurent Nkunda. Among the violations reported were sexual assaults, deaths, displacements and attacks.

In conclusion, mobile phones are, and will remain a great tool for human rights and health activism. This, however, does not mitigate the damage caused by the exploitation of raw materials such as coltan used in their manufacture. The success achieved thus far inspires hope and points to the potential for the use of mobile telephony in other social, economic and political spheres, especially in elections.

One of the questions posed by the project was whether there could be a link between the drop in cases and the use of mobile phones? It would be impossible to tell for sure, but one can say that the organisation did meet its objectives – to ensure the timely reporting of children's rights violations and the appropriate responses – judging by the results. Nonetheless the fact remains that SMS technology may be cheap, but it is not easy to use for many of those living in the rural areas. In the AJEDI-Ka/PES project, for instance, there were no reports submitted by SMS. The main reasons why the informants preferred not to use SMS were: it is time-consuming and there is no guarantee that the receiver will read the message; the limited number of characters one can use may not be sufficient to communicate the message; and many people are unable to navigate the SMS functions on their mobile phones. The Ushahidi case is a good example of the limitations of SMS in zones of crisis. The number of reports was less than had been hoped. Again one reason may have been the reliance on SMS as opposed to voice. As Ory Okolloh comments on 'issues specific to crisis situations':

> As one person closely involved in assisting people affected by the crisis in DRC pointed out to me, in a crisis situation most people are on the run – they don't have time to file reports etc.

In a place like eastern DRC that is compounded by things like electricity cuts so phones can't be charged [and] difficulties having the resources to buy credit so the SMS functionality doesn't really help them.[5]

The use of mobile phones for children's rights activism is well suited to environments facing challenges such as poor network coverage, technical deficiencies and costs. The mobile phone networks have also introduced a range of products that offer internet access wherever one may be. In the context of the present monitoring and reporting project, it is even conceivable that the reports could be sent directly from the villages where the violations are committed to the United Nations, via Watchlist on Children and Armed Conflict.

Notes

1. AJEDI-Ka/Projet Enfants Soldats, 'Monitoring and reporting on child rights violations', http://www.ajedika.org/reports.html, accessed 16 September 2009.
2. Ajedi-Ka/Projet Enfants Soldats, 'Rapport Sur Les Violations des Droits des Enfants dans le Territoire D'Uvira et de Fizi, Sud-Kivu, RDC'.
3. Crowdsourcing crisis mapping software platform, www.ushahidi.com.
4. Ushahidi DRC Map, http://drc.ushahidi.com/, accessed 18 June 2009.
5. Okolloh, O. (2008) 'Covering the DRC: challenges of Ushahidi', http://blog.ushahidi.com/index.php/2008/12/03/covering-the-drc-challenges-for-ushahidi/, accessed 19 September 2009.

Appendix: Resources

Websites

Connect Africa – http://connectafrica.wordpress.com
DigiActive – http://www.digiactive.org
Hello Africa – ICT4D – http://wiki.ict4d.at/Hello_Africa
Kabissa – http://www.kabissa.org
Mobile Active – http://www.mobileactive08.org
Mobile Applications Database – http://www.kiwanja.net/database/kiwanja_search.php
Ushahidi – http://www.ushahidi.com
Movirtu – http://www.movirtu.com
Smart Mobs – http://www.smartmobs.com
Textually – http://www.textually.org/Services
Mixit – http://www.mxit.com
Sembuse – http://m.sembuse.com

African related technology blogs

AfriGadget – http://www.afrigadget.com
Afrigator – http://www.afrigator.com
Afromusing – http://afromusing.com
AppFrica – http://appfrica.net/blog
Crisscrossed – http://www.crisscrossed.net
Kiwanja – http://www.kiwanja.net
Tactical Tech – http://www.tacticaltech.org
'White African' – http://www.whiteafrican.com

Index

More books from Pambazuka Press

Available at www.pambazukapress.org

Aid to Africa: Redeemer or Coloniser?

Edited by Hakima Abbas and Yves Niyiragira

This book offers a critical analysis of aid to Africa. The authors examine the framework of aid from 'traditional' Western donors while investigating how the emergence of new donors to Africa has changed the international aid discourse and architecture. The uniquely African perspectives in this book provide both a framework for 'reforming' aid and an alternative development paradigm rooted in Africa's self-determination. Contributing authors to this volume include Samir Amin, Patrick Bond and Demba Moussa Dembélé.

ISBN: 978-1-906387-38-9 · July 2009 · £12.95 · 204pp

Development and Globalisation
Daring to Think Differently

Yash Tandon

This book challenges the misdirected policies of the last 30 years. It offers alternative concepts and paradigms of development for policy makers and peoples' movements on wide-ranging issues. It invites readers to 'dare to think differently'. According to the author, development is self-defined. It is primarily the responsibility of the South to develop itself; the North does not have a duty to develop the South, nor should the South expect it. Development is about building confidence between governments and people and not building confidence with banks and global financial institutions such as the World Bank and the IMF, which is what globalisation is all about.

Yash Tandon is a professor of political economy and the former executive director of the South Centre, Geneva.

ISBN: 978-1-906387-51-8 · October 2009 · £9.95

Food Rebellions!
Crisis and the Hunger for Justice

Eric Holt-Giménez and Raj Patel

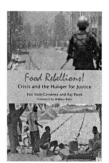

Food Rebellions! takes a deep look at the world food crisis and its impact on the global South and underserved communities in the industrial North. While most governments and multilateral organisations offer short-term solutions based on proximate causes, authors Eric Holt-Giménez and Raj Patel unpack the planet's environmentally and economically vulnerable food systems to reveal the root causes of the crisis.

Eric Holt-Giménez is the executive director of Food First – Institute for Food and Development Policy in Oakland, California.

Raj Patel is the acclaimed author of *Stuffed and Starved: Markets, Power and the Hidden Battle for the World Food System* (2007).

ISBN: 978-1-906387-30-3 · July 2009 · £16.95 · 256pp

Where is Uhuru?
Reflections on the Struggle for Democracy in Africa

Issa G. Shivji

Edited by Godwin R. Murunga

The neoliberal project promised to engender development and prosperity and expand democratic space in Africa. However, several decades on its reforms have delivered on few of its promises. Whether one is examining the rewards of multiparty politics, the dividends from a new constitutional dispensation, the processes of land reform, women's rights to property or the pan-Africanist project for emancipation, Issa G. Shivji illustrates how these have all suffered severe body blows. Where, indeed, is Uhuru?

Issa G. Shivji is the Mwalimu Nyerere Professor of Pan-African Studies at the University of Dar es Salaam and the author of *The Concept of Human Rights in Africa* (1989).

ISBN: 978-1-906387-46-4 · April 2009 · £16.95 · 257pp

LaVergne, TN USA
07 October 2010
199935LV00002B/1/P